COL OG NE

Travel with Marco Polo Insider Tips

INSIDER TIP
Your shortcut to a great experience

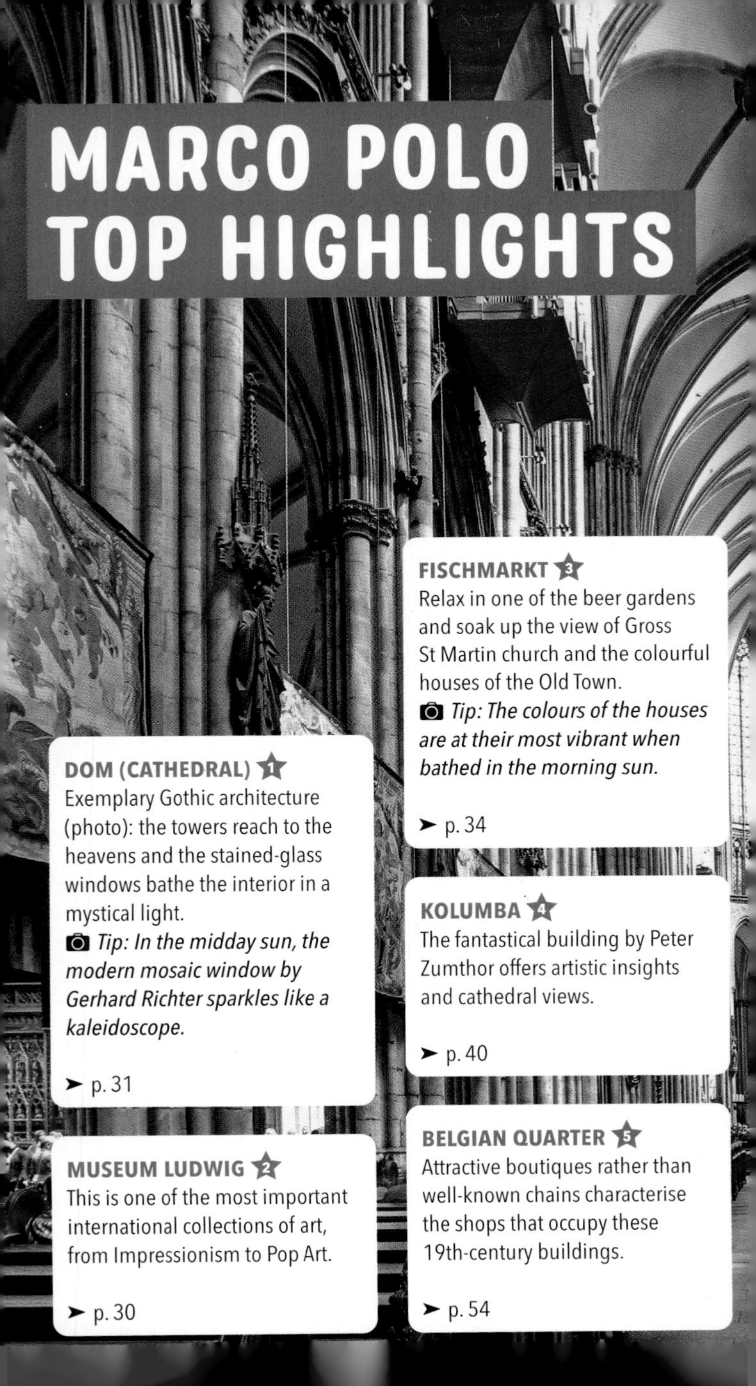

MARCO POLO
TOP HIGHLIGHTS

FISCHMARKT ★
Relax in one of the beer gardens and soak up the view of Gross St Martin church and the colourful houses of the Old Town.
📷 *Tip: The colours of the houses are at their most vibrant when bathed in the morning sun.*

➤ p. 34

DOM (CATHEDRAL) ★
Exemplary Gothic architecture (photo): the towers reach to the heavens and the stained-glass windows bathe the interior in a mystical light.
📷 *Tip: In the midday sun, the modern mosaic window by Gerhard Richter sparkles like a kaleidoscope.*

➤ p. 31

KOLUMBA ★
The fantastical building by Peter Zumthor offers artistic insights and cathedral views.

➤ p. 40

MUSEUM LUDWIG ★
This is one of the most important international collections of art, from Impressionism to Pop Art.

➤ p. 30

BELGIAN QUARTER ★
Attractive boutiques rather than well-known chains characterise the shops that occupy these 19th-century buildings.

➤ p. 54

RHEINTREPPE ✪

The years of construction were worth it; now you can enjoy the river in the sun with a great view.
📷 *Tip: For the perfect picture, make your way to the east end of the Hohenzollern bridge at dusk.*

➤ p. 45

RHEINAUHAFEN ✪

The city's most successful urban development project has created boulevards, restaurants and convivial corners.

➤ p. 50

EHRENFELD ✪

The nightclubs in Cologne's hipster district create a party zone at weekends.
📷 *Tip: Take the metro to Leyendeckerstrasse; the station's impressive lighting is an attraction in itself.*

➤ p. 53

INNERER GRÜNGÜRTEL ✪

The city's youth love to meet up here, especially in good weather.
📷 *Tip: The atmosphere at the Aachener Weiher lake on a summer evening is reminiscent of a beach party.*

➤ p. 55

CARNIVAL ✪

Semi-pedestrianised Chlodwigplatz is the epicentre of the annual revels.

➤ p. 102

CONTENTS

⏱	Plan your visit	☂	Rainy day activities
€–€€€	Price categories	🐷	Budget activities
(*)	Premium-rate phone number	👪	Family activities
		🚩	Classic experiences

(📖 A2) Refers to the removable pull-out map
(0) Located off the map

CONTENTS

BEST OF
COLOGNE

All aboard! A boat trip on the Rhine is an essential Cologne experience

BEST ☂ WHEN IT RAINS

ACTIVITIES TO BRIGHTEN YOUR DAY

FROM PICASSO TO POP ART

Museum Ludwig has masterpieces from the past 100 years in its permanent collection, as well as changing exhibitions showcasing the most important artists and influences in modern and contemporary art. The Picasso collection is the third-largest in the world (photo).

➤ p. 30

MUSEUM DUO

Whatever the weather, you won't get bored in the *Kulturzentrum Neumarkt*. The *Rautenstrauch-Joest Museum* takes you on a journey around the world, starting with the huge rice store in the foyer. Follow that by visiting the sacred treasures in the *Schnütgen Museum*.

➤ p. 39

BROWSE THE VINYL

The *Underdog Recordstore* is one of the best record shops in Germany. There's enough stuff to get you through an entire rainy weekend, and the vinyl treasures are reasonably priced too.

➤ p. 81

LUXURY CINEMA

Enjoy endless legroom in comfortable chairs, while you're served tapas and a bottle of wine for two. At the *Residenz Astor Film Lounge*, going to the movies is fun again. There are special screenings for classic films too.

➤ p. 96

GOLF WITH A DIFFERENCE

The mini-golf course at the *Glowing Rooms* in Ehrenfeld is a bit special: you play under "black light" on greens and fairways that you can only see when you put on the 3D glasses. Beer is available, but it may not help your putting skills…

➤ p. 100

BEST ON A BUDGET

FOR SMALLER WALLETS

UNFORGETTABLE CATHEDRAL SOUNDS
The choral concerts in the cathedral's Shrine of the Three Kings and the summer organ recitals are musical experiences not to be missed.
➤ p. 32

PALM TREES IN PRIDE OF PLACE
The newly renovated *Botanic Garden* is worth a visit, not least for the avenue of Chinese windmill palms – the most northerly of its kind in Europe (photo).
➤ p. 52

A GREEN OASIS WITH FREE ART
A manicured lawn is the setting for the *Skulpturenpark*, where around 30 sculptures by renowned artists such as Louise Bourgeois or Martin Kippenberger are displayed. The exhibited works are changed every two years.
➤ p. 53

CLASSICAL FLAVOURS
Enjoy a musical accompaniment to your lunch break with *Philharmonie-Lunch*. The Gürzenich Orchestra and the WDR Symphony Orchestra take it in turns to perform under the watchful eye of the conductor.
➤ p. 95

FINE DESIGN
Passagen Interior Design Week enlivens the city with events, cocktail parties and concerts – from classical to hard rock. *Design Parcours Ehrenfeld* is the focal point for events.
➤ p. 102

SUMMER PARTIES
A "singing beer garden", theatre acts from all over the world, concerts, artists and puppet shows: the open-air *Sommer Köln* programme takes place in parks and squares all over the city, and admission is free.
➤ p. 103

BEST WITH CHILDREN

FUN FOR YOUNG & OLD

COLOGNE FROM ABOVE

Wow! Children and their grown-ups are amazed by the panoramic views of the cathedral, the city and the countryside beyond from the 103m-high viewing platform of the *Köln Triangle*.
➤ p. 45

HIGH ABOVE THE RHINE

Taking the *cable car* (photo) over the river is an experience not to be missed. You travel in wonderfully old-fashioned cabins with a view of the city skyline. At the terminus, there's fun to be had at either the zoo or the *Rheinpark*.
➤ p. 46

CHOCOLATE CENTRAL

The *Schokoladenmuseum* offers an entertaining insight into the whole chocolate production process, from the cacao plants in the greenhouse to the packaging. Highlight: the chocolate fondue in the adjoining café.
➤ p. 49

FEED THE DEER

Cologne has plenty of green space – and the *Wildgehege im Stadtwald* (city forest nature reserve) in particular is a world apart from the city's bustle. And with deer to feed by hand, the forest idyll is complete.
➤ p. 55

A BREAK FROM THE CITY

There's plenty of room for kids to run about and fly kites on the *Poller Wiesen* (meadows). More of a surprise is the *Strandbar (poller-strandbar.de)*, where they can swim and play on the small beach.
➤ p. 56

PLAY & PICNIC

The *Volksgarten* is a lovely park close to the city centre, where kids can let off steam. The beer garden provides welcome sustenance for both adults and children.
➤ p. 62

BEST 🚩

CLASSIC EXPERIENCES

ONLY IN COLOGNE

IS IT A BIRD?
Order *"ne Halve Hahn"* (half a chicken) in a *Brauhaus* but don't be surprised when you are served a rye roll and cheese. For the most authentic version of this snack with the confusing name, visit *Früh am Dom*.
➤ p. 62

SPEAKING & DRINKING KÖLSCH
Kölsch is a dialect *and* a drink. The local hoppy, light beer is served in small 200ml glasses, *Stangen*, so it stays cold and fresh. Try out your language and your drinking skills at the *Schreckenskammer*, which brews its own Kölsch.
➤ p. 63

COLOGNE-STYLE CUSTOMER SERVICE
The *Köbes* (traditional Cologne waiting staff) are an institution in local gastronomy and belong to the folklore of Cologne's brewery pubs. To find out just how witty and gruff (and rude!) they can be, visit *Päffgen*.
➤ p. 63

PUPPET PLAYS
You probably won't understand what's going on, but you can still appreciate the spectacle and skill of the *Puppenspiele der Stadt Köln* (photo) – the official name of the Hänneschen Puppet Theatre. It presents satirical plays in Kölsch, the local dialect, that lampoon current events.
➤ p. 96

THREE DAYS OF FUN
The traditional Kölsch saying promises "Three days of fun, no regrets – that is carnival". Join the masked revellers at Cologne's carnival street parades and experience one of the traditions that shape the city's identity.
➤ p. 102

GET TO KNOW COLOGNE

Everyone joins in the carnival fun

DISCOVER COLOGNE

It's only a short hop from the Rhine to the Altstadt

Cologne doesn't reveal all its charms at first glance. But anyone who takes the time to get to know the city will discover a lively metropolis with an unmistakable character that goes beyond the clichés. It is relatively compact compared to other German cities, which makes it ideal for exploration on foot or by bike.

MORE THAN MEETS THE EYE

The cathedral. The Rhine. A few glasses of Kölsch. And carnival, of course. Cologne is happy for its reputation to be defined by these four cornerstones. Traditionalists might argue that there's not much else to the city. Even the beloved FC Cologne

38 BCE
The Romans found a settlement in the area that will become Colonia Agrippina.

c CE 310
The population of Roman Cologne grows to 15,000. Emperor Constantine commissions the first bridge over the Rhine.

1248
Construction of the cathedral begins. Cologne is granted "staple rights" – all goods shipped on the river must be unloaded and offered for sale in the city before they are traded elsewhere.

1709
Perfumer Johann Maria Farina invents eau de Cologne.

has become so professional and grown-up that supporting the team is almost a little boring. To be honest, the same could be said of the city itself, if you were to judge it by its official image. It may be sufficient to keep Cologne natives happy, and it certainly gives visitors reason enough to visit, but it's not the whole story: there are, in reality, many sides to Cologne.

THE CATHEDRAL AND ITS SHADOW

There's no doubt that the massive religious monument, the slow-moving river, the restrained portions of beer, and the wild carnival parades are vital to the city's identity. But Cologne's real appeal lies elsewhere: it is one of the world's most compact cities, with a population of over one million. Travel between the city's varied districts is quick and easy. Cologne is over 2,000 years old, but it's barely 5km between the Romanesque churches in the city's historic district and the Ehrenfeld industrial area. In fact, Ehrenfeld exemplifies a side of Cologne that river cruise passengers and bus tourists never see. Obviously, you'd be hard-pressed to find "tourist sights" here, at least in the traditional sense of the term. But Ehrenfeld is home to a number of modern subcultures. Young people from all over the world gather here, especially at weekends. Ultra-hip Ehrenfeld clubs like Bumann & Sohn are not only the envy of Berlin, they're also attracting growing numbers of people who speak English, Spanish and Dutch. Cologne has partying in its blood – thanks to carnival, of course.

1823
The first Shrove Monday procession takes place in Cologne, making it the oldest carnival in Germany.

1880
Cologne Cathedral is finally completed.

1939–45
Up to 90 per cent of the city is destroyed during World War II.

2009
The city archive collapses during work on the underground travel system.

2022
After 12 years of delays, the city authorities announce that the renovation of the will be ready for the 2024/25 season ....

CHAIN-FREE SHOPPING

And if it's the hippest spots you're after, the Belgian Quarter (Belgisches Viertel) is another must. When Cologne's city walls came down in the late 19th century, the city expanded into this area; between Venloer, Brüsseler and Aachener streets, you can still experience some of the charm of that era, which was lost to the bombs of World War II in most of the rest of the city. The ruins were replaced by functional buildings with tiled façades – the architecture still irritates proponents of conventional aesthetics to this day, but it has found new fans among the hip younger generation. You'll find the city's coolest shops in the Belgian Quarter: record shops, little boutiques with carefully chosen collections, vintage shops, design specialists and other purveyors of necessities for the modern urban lifestyle. So far, the global chain stores haven't encroached beyond the main Cologne ring road.

There's another thing you can find in the Belgian Quarter today: bananas on the façades of the buildings. The street art images were created by Cologne-based artist Thomas Baumgärtel to identify galleries. After hitting a low point with the mass exodus of artists to the unavoidable art mecca of Berlin, the Cologne art scene is vibrant once again. In fact, fine art is another good reason to visit Cologne. The city has two top-rated art museums: Museum Ludwig and the Wallraf (Richartz) Museum.

ARCHITECTURAL TREASURES

Downtown, however, are visible remnants of ancient history. Sure, there's the cathedral, but it's not really that old: it wasn't actually completed until 1880, following a hiatus in construction that lasted for over three centuries. In light of that history, the countless mishaps that have delayed both the construction of the subway line to the southern part of town and the renovation of the opera house and theatre don't seem all that dramatic. Yet, in the medieval parts of Cologne, Romanesque churches serve as a reminder of the city's staunchly Catholic past. There are a dozen of them; they often go unnoticed, but each one has its own history and architectural merit: a cloister here, a rose garden there.

An awe-inspiring reminder of the past is located deeper under the earth: the Praetorium is a former Roman governor's palace from the fourth century CE. However, due to construction of the Museums im Quartier (MiQua), this historical site is likely to remain inaccessible until at least 2025.

KÖLSCH REIGNS SUPREME

Here, right next to the cathedral and the Rhine, is where the spirit of Cologne was born. The best place to find that spirit today is in the Old Town brewpubs, where the Kölsch flows freely and where obscure (but delicious) dishes, such as *Himmel un Äd* ("heaven and earth" – mashed potatoes and black pudding), *Halve Hahn* ("half a chicken" – cheese roll) and *Hämchen* (ham hock), are served. These are

No question: you *have* to drink Kölsch in a Cologne brewhouse

the workplaces of the infamous *Köbesse* – specialist brewhouse waiters who bring refills of beer without being asked. Your *Köbe* might make a snarky comment if you order a non-alcoholic drink, but if you ask him to join you for a beer, he'll be happy to oblige. The brewhouses are always sociable places. And the best beers (Päffgen and Mühlen) can justly claim to use the same brewing principles and ingredients that are reserved for so-called "craft beers" in other cities.

LIFE LESSONS AND SEASONAL SONGS

As the city expanded, so the number of brewhouses increased, meaning that wherever you go in Cologne, you will find one where you can learn a few of the city's guiding principles in the local dialect: *Et kütt wie et kütt* ("What will be, will be"), *Jeder Jeck ist anders* ("Every fool is different" – an early expression of tolerance), or *Wat fott es, es fott* ("What's gone is gone" – or, there's no point crying over spilt milk). These simple rules still shape the Cologne mentality, even in the third millennium.

Local songs are also near and dear to the hearts of Cologne natives, and the collection of those tunes is constantly growing. Carnival always generates lots of new songs (not to mention truckloads of euros for the top-ranking bands). The most important source is the carnival song contest known as *Loss mer singe* ("Let's sing"), which tours the entire region during the carnival season; it separates the wheat from the chaff to find the next top hits for the coming festivities.

Anyone who's ever joined in the contest knows that it can be nearly impossible to get those songs out of your head. And the songs essentially have one message: Cologne is the most beautiful, liveable and tolerant city on the planet.

COMPACT AND CUTTING EDGE

Many inhabitants of Cologne believe that their city's hoard of carnival songs represents a meaningful contribution to the heritage of the nation. Others believe that Cologne's most important musical achievements lie elsewhere (although that doesn't diminish the value of carnival, of course!). After all, Cologne is also the birthplace of the record label *Kompakt*, which exported minimalist techno from the banks of the Rhine to the rest of the world; some theorists suggest this marked a worthy conclusion to musical history. Techno culture remains prominent in the Cologne's club scene.

In general, the city highly prizes research, technology and modernity. Fifty thousand students attend the University of Cologne alone; many more study at the city's other colleges. Companies including Microsoft and Electronic Arts have their German headquarters in one of the most desirable areas of Cologne: the Rheinauhafen.

The concentration of innovation in a relatively small urban area is balanced by the city's two green belts, the inner and the outer. If you choose the right routes, you can move around the city for a whole day avoiding main roads. For a long time, the priority given to car traffic and the resulting prevalence of tarmac were two of the city's greatest weaknesses. Recently, however, more and more parking spaces are being removed in favour of outdoor eating areas, while former roads are giving way to cycle paths. The result is a patchwork of green and asphalt – but at least it's a start.

JOIN IN THE FUN

But visitors shouldn't let the inconsistencies bother them; they should simply enjoy what the city has to offer – thrilling nightlife, a high concentration of restaurants, evidence of a deeply rooted local culture and the presence of subcultures that are constantly reinventing themselves. Let the day gently glide away as you relax in the green belt or in the cafés of the Belgian Quarter. Maybe plan your visit around one of the events that engulfs the whole city in frenetic excitement: the Passagen exhibitions during the International Interior Design Show, Art Cologne, or the c/o pop music festival. But just because you're attending a cutting-edge event doesn't mean you should neglect tradition: sing along with all the traditional songs during the carnival season, take a stroll along the Rhine, or cheer on FC Cologne alongside the hometown fans. Soak up the atmosphere every time the home team scores a goal, when the traditional song *(Wenn et Trömmelche jeht)* rings out around the stadium. You could even share a Kölsch with the fans to celebrate a big win. *Prost!*

AT A GLANCE

1,090,000
inhabitants

Birmingham: 1,141,400

16
breweries

produce bottled Kölsch

**AREA:
405km²**

Birmingham: 268km²

414,800
Number of residents with an
immigrant background

Largest group: roughly 94,000
have Turkish roots

**TALLEST BUILDING:
COLONIUS TV TOWER**

266m

London's BT Tower
177m

**MOST POPULAR TIME
TO VISIT:**

THE "FIFTH SEASON"

**11 November until
Ash Wednesday**

**NUMBER OF
ROMANESQUE
CHURCHES**

12

10 BILLION EUROS

The cost of building Cologne cathedral in today's figures

400m

The length of Zülpicher Strasse, known as
the "Party Mile"

FAMOUS PEOPLE FROM COLOGNE:
KONRAD ADENAUER (FIRST
CHANCELLOR OF WEST GERMANY)
HEINRICH BÖLL (NOVELIST)
NICO (SINGER)
GOKHAN TORE (FOOTBALLER)

UNDERSTAND COLOGNE

CELEBRATE CARNIVAL IN THE RIGHT WAY

It may be a cliché, but Cologne's image is inextricably linked to its carnival. Outsiders may have good reason to be sceptical – but the temptation to dive head first into the fun usually wins out. However, caution is required; newbies may have the best of intentions, but it's easy to make mistakes. Remember: for a successful carnival experience, the most important thing is patience. Take it slow – and that applies to alcohol, too. There's ample time to party; the revelry carries on into the wee hours of the morning, and you can join in at any time. Pro tip: carnival veterans only drink Kölsch and water and avoid the harder stuff.

Of course, choosing the right bar or venue is even more important. It's best to ask trustworthy locals where they go to celebrate during the carnival season. Or look for the pubs with the longest queues at the door. The southern part of the city *(Backes, Darmstädter Str. 6 | backeskoeln.de)* and the Eigelstein district *(Anno Pief, Im Stavenhof 8 | anno-pief.de)* are excellent places to find bars and venues offering an authentic carnival experience. Zülpicher Strasse, on the other hand, is to be avoided.

Be aware that queuing is part of the ritual: if you want to party properly, plan for two hours of standing out in the cold. You'll make your first local friends in that queue, guaranteed! And, as time goes on, you may be tempted to start thinking of the carnival atmosphere (and your new costumed friends) as part of your new reality. But bear in mind the hard and fast rule in Cologne: the festivities always end by Ash Wednesday, and they don't start up again until 11 November. Enjoy the party, the music, the costumes and every other aspect of carnival while it lasts, and when it's all over, don't be sad – just remember that there's always next year!

INSIDER TIP
Takeaway beer is essential

COMEDY GOLD

Cologne's carnival is at least partially responsible for the number of comedians in the city. Carolin Kebekus, one of Germany's biggest comedy stars, never baulked at the opportunity to entertain revellers (and make them think!) during carnival season as she began her meteoric rise to comedy fame. Like many of her colleagues, she's a welcome guest at the *Cologne Comedy Festival (koelncomedy.de)* in October, at which the industry's most important award, the Deutscher Comedypreis, is awarded. Comedians – from local stars to national celebrities – bring the laughs at more than 20 venues throughout the city. Who says Germans have no sense of humour?

EAU DE COLOGNE

The production of this distillation of alcohol and blossom oil started in

Up to 1.5 million spectators watch the Rosenmontag parade

1709. The secret recipe was passed on to Wilhelm Mülhens in 1792 as a wedding gift and was originally marketed as a miracle cure for headaches, heart palpitations and even to ward off the plague. When, in 1810, Napoleon demanded the disclosure of all medicinal formulas, Mülhens was only able to keep his recipe secret by marketing it as a fragrance with refreshing qualities. In 1794, a general in the occupying French army had all the buildings in Cologne numbered. Wilhelm Mülhens' home in the Glockengasse was given the number 4711. This house number is in use to this day. Pop into the *Dufthaus 4711* and refresh yourself at the eau de Cologne fountain.

COLOGNE'S VEEDELS

There is a song by the local band Bläck Fööss – often sung at official commemorative events – that says that the most important thing in life is your *Veedel*, or your neighbourhood. This song epitomises the special sentimentality of the Cologne sense of belonging. People's strong identification with their own neighbourhood gives them a sense of belonging that offers a calming influence and a haven from an otherwise incomprehensible and stormy world. This sentiment applies to every district of the city, regardless of its social status, from expensive residential areas like Marienburg, to peaceful suburbs like Dellbrück and the multicultural Eigelstein district.

CAR-MAKERS & CREATIVES

Cologne was once a major manufacturing hub, but very few traces of its industrial past remain in the city centre. Just a few kilometres outside the city, however – in Leverkusen, Hürth and Wesseling – enormous (petro) chemical plants still loom over the skyline. And in Cologne proper, the Ford plant (founded in 1929) remains as a reminder of the city's blue-collar heritage. The largest employers in the city today are the REWE retail group, with over 22,000 employees, Ford (14,000 employees but with lay-offs expected) and the city utilities (including transport, 13,000 employees).

Outwardly, the city remains proudest of its creative industries. Even in this era of declining print journalism, the city is still a media metropolis, with production companies and internet start-ups all finding a home here.

LET'S SING!

Music sung in local dialects might be off-putting for some, but the local Cologne version is definitely worth a try – especially since these days, younger artists are also getting in on the act, singing the praises of Cologne and its cathedral. Some noteworthy names among this new generation of performers are Miljö, who sing about the Lommerzheim pub in Deutz; Kasalla, especially their hit song "Pirate"; and Cat Ballou, whose song "*Et jitt kei Wood*" claims that "there are no words" to explain the love they feel for their hometown. Veteran bartenders have been spotted openly weeping, so moved were they

It's not all Kölsch and Karneval: Weidengasse in the Eigelstein district ITINA

by these odes to Cologne. The Cologne song contest, *Loss mer singe (loss mersinge.de)*, is partially responsible for this boom; this is where the songs with the greatest potential are chosen to become the hits of the carnival season.

LIVE & LET LIVE

Intolerance, xenophobia and hatred of any kind are not welcome in Cologne. Far-right political parties and other organisations with similar ideologies don't get a good reception here. The local initiative *Arsch huh, Zäng ussenander* ("Get off your arse, speak up") regularly campaigns against the far right, largely with the vocal support of the general public. This open-minded attitude is one of the reasons why Cologne is regarded as safe space for the LGBTQ+ community.

The city adheres to a "live and let live" philosophy that has served it well over the years. And it's more than just hot air; it's a tried-and-tested model. There aren't many regulations in Cologne: clubs, bars and pubs can stay open as late as they like; barbecuing in the park is considered a normal activity; parking violations result in only small fines; and if the neighbours are playing a new TV series at top volume, the correct Cologne response is to shrug and mutter "*Jeder Jeck es anders*". It seems to work pretty well – partly because the city has a budget for cleaning up its public spaces. But the pre-requisite for such relaxed attitudes is that the majority of the population sticks to the city's unwritten rules.

TRUE OR FALSE?

COLOGNE IS A SENTIMENTAL CITY

Cologne is the most beautiful, most tolerant and most lovable city in the world – bar none. This opinion is expressed by residents whenever they get together for a drink and is also reflected in the lyrics of the most popular local songs. Visit a corner pub even early in the day, and there's a good chance you'll see tears welling up in the eyes of the bar-maids when they hear the mawkish tones of "Stääne" by Klüngelköpp coming out of the speakers. The diagnosis: the people of Cologne suffer from incurable sentimentality.

YOU CAN ONLY DRINK KÖLSCH IN COLOGNE

Kölsch is a characterless beer drunk out of ridiculously small glasses. This is the opinion of many other Germans – particularly Bavarians – regarding the Rhineland's own amber nectar. How wrong they are! Although the name "Kölsch" is protected in Germany and production is restricted to the area immediately around Cologne, Kölsch is experiencing a boom among beer-drinkers abroad – especially in English-speaking countries, such as Australia and the USA. They prize the top-fermented beer's lightness and drinkability – even if they drink it out of glasses that are far too big!

NETWORKING OR CRONYISM?

What is known as "networking" in the rest of the world is a historically entrenched form of cronyism known as *Klüngel* in Cologne. It's an opaque and complex mesh of personal relations with mutual benefits. You scratch my back and I'll scratch yours. This tendency towards behind-the-scenes wheeling and dealing developed over the centuries as the city successfully resisted all unwanted influences from penetrating its walls. (Given this history, Cologne natives of the older generation must find it very odd that public job vacancies now have to be advertised throughout Europe as a matter of course.) The Cologne *Klüngel* had a last hurrah at the beginning of the new millennium, with the scandal-ridden construction of both the new Cologne trade fair site and the local waste incineration plant; but, since then, *Klüngel* seems to have met its match in today's anti-corruption laws. Occasionally, however, politicians of all stripes still attempt (sometimes successfully) to get themselves lucrative jobs in public institutions without due process.

MEDIA CITY

Cologne's art and media college *(Kunsthochschule für Medien)* is unique in Germany and is indicative of Cologne's status as a media city. Almost a third of all television programmes by Germany's largest regional public broadcaster WDR are produced in Cologne, with many TV crime scenes filmed on the city's streets. You can visit the studios and outdoor locations on a *free tour (2 hrs | wdr.de)*. WDR accounts for 4,500 coveted jobs in the city, and other important broadcasters such as Deutschlandradio and the RTL Group – which includes channels such as Vox, Super RTL and NTV news – are also based in Cologne.

PROBLEM AREAS

Cologne has grown organically over the centuries. Each district has its own unique character, and the distances between them are relatively short for a city of over one million inhabitants. This makes it ideal for cyclists, pedestrians and public transport. Politicians and the city's administration have at last recognised this fact. But, since the car has been the priority for decades, it is a considerable challenge to reclaim public spaces in favour of other modes of transport. The city is gradually turning roads into cycle paths and car parks into public spaces for outdoor eating, but the bike paths often end abruptly or are interrupted by traffic intersections. In this way, the city has become a patchwork, rather than a network, of alternative transport solutions. But there is hope. One example is Zülpicher Strasse, much of which is closed to cars, which means you can join the picnicking students on the tarmac outside the university canteen to eat your lunch or dinner.

INSIDER TIP Street picnic

Cars have even been banned from much-loved Ehrenstrasse. However, that doesn't mean that serious shoppers can stroll around undisturbed;

Check out the striking architecture of the WDR shopping arcade in the city centre

cyclists can still use the street, which leads to new conflicts with pedestrians. Nevertheless, the measures that have been implemented so far ensure that the dream of a traffic-free city centre lives on; it is hoped that as more and more streets become part of the scheme, the problems will diminish.

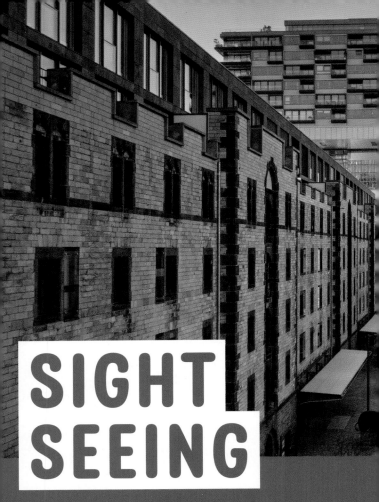

SIGHT SEEING

The cathedral, the Old Town, the Romanesque churches, the banks of the Rhine, the fantastic museums, the brewhouses and the carnival: these are Cologne's main tourist attractions, but they're only one side of the city. Cologne has the self-confidence to believe that it's just as hip as Hamburg or Berlin – it's just a little more compact.

The clubs in Ehrenfeld are among the best in Europe. The bars and cafés in the Belgian Quarter are varied and stylish. It's possible to

All the venues in this chapter can be found on the pull-out map 📖

The *Kranhäuser* are an iconic landmark in the hip *Rheinauhafen* district

shop till you drop in Germany's fourth-largest city without setting foot in a global chain store; spend your euros on vinyl and vintage clothing instead. New trends are adopted quickly, or even started here, because Cologne is home to a large number of students and creatives. All these advantages mean that the city's neighbourhoods are its real attraction; fortunately, the south of the city (Südstadt), the Belgian Quarter, the Agnes Quarter and Ehrenfeld can all be reached quickly by bike or bus from the city centre.

NEIGHBOURHOOD OVERVIEW

MARCO POLO HIGHLIGHTS

★ **MUSEUM LUDWIG**
The third-largest Picasso collection in the world ➤ p. 30

★ **DOM (CATHEDRAL)**
Cologne's landmark cathedral has long been a UNESCO World Heritage Site ➤ p. 31

★ **FISCHMARKT**
A pretty square with picturesque gabled houses and welcoming beer gardens ➤ p. 34

★ **WALLRAF-RICHARTZ MUSEUM & FONDATION CORBOUD**
Paintings from the Middle Ages up to the Impressionist era ➤ p. 37

★ **KOLUMBA**
The Museum of the Archdiocese of Cologne doesn't sound very appealing – but the building is stunning and the collection is fascinating ➤ p. 40

★ **RHEINTREPPE**
A gorgeous outdoor spot, especially at sunset ➤ p. 45

★ **ST URSULA**
An eerie monument to the medieval cult of relics ➤ p. 48

★ **RHEINAUHAFEN**
Youthful, hip and with cutting-edge architecture ➤ p. 50

★ **EHRENFELD**
Check out the innovative underground club scene in the city's hippest district ➤ p. 53

★ **BELGIAN QUARTER**
Hip independent boutiques are clustered around Aachener Strasse ➤ p. 54

★ **INNERER GRÜNGÜRTEL**
Meeting point and green oasis on the edge of the city centre ➤ p. 55

CITY CENTRE p. 38
Shops and museums dominate this area outside the Old Town but inside the ring road

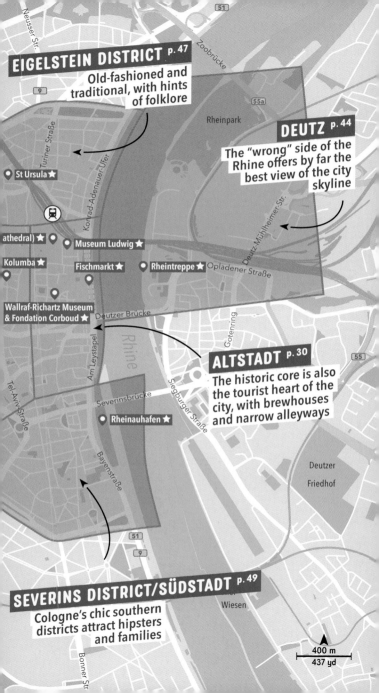

EIGELSTEIN DISTRICT p. 47
Old-fashioned and traditional, with hints of folklore

DEUTZ p. 44
The "wrong" side of the Rhine offers by far the best view of the city skyline

St Ursula ★

athedral) ★   Museum Ludwig ★

Kolumba ★   Fischmarkt ★   Rheintreppe ★

Wallraf-Richartz Museum & Fondation Corboud ★

ALTSTADT p. 30
The historic core is also the tourist heart of the city, with brewhouses and narrow alleyways

Rheinauhafen ★

SEVERINS DISTRICT/SÜDSTADT p. 49
Cologne's chic southern districts attract hipsters and families

Rheinpark

Rhine

Deutzer Friedhof

Wiesen

400 m
437 yd

Neusser Str.
Zoobrücke
55a
Turiner Straße
Konrad-Adenauer-Ufer
Deutz-Mühlheimer-Str.
Opladener Straße
Deutzer Brücke
Am Leystapel
Tel-Aviv-Straße
Severinsbrücke
Siegburger Straße
Gotenring
Bayenstraße
Bonner Str.
51
9
55

ALTSTADT

Nestled around the perfectly proportioned church of Gross St Martin are the winding streets, rustic brewhouses and pretty gabled houses that characterise the *Altstadt* (Old Town).

Tourists in search of refreshment, after marvelling at the cathedral or the museums, wander through streets that have changed considerably over the centuries. The area was renovated and sanitised in the 1930s, completely destroyed during World War II and then reconstructed in the years that followed. In the 1970s city leaders promoted the development of the area as a pub district – in order to compete with the Altstadt in Düsseldorf, which boasted that it was the "longest bar in the world".

WHERE TO START?

Dom (Cathedral) *(◫ G4)*: on the metro, take lines U 5, 16 or 18 to Dom/Hbf (Hauptbahnhof – the main station); by car, head for the Dom car park (entrances on Trankgasse and at the end of the underpass Am Domhof/Kurt-Hackenberg-Platz) or the Dom/Rhein car park (entrance on Grosse Neugasse). Here, you'll be in the heart of the Altstadt and the shopping district that begins on Wallrafplatz/Hohe Strasse. It's a seven-minute walk north on Marzellenstrasse to the Eigelstein district, or a ten-minute walk from the cathedral to the right bank of the Rhine in Deutz, via the Hohenzollern Bridge.

1 MUSEUM LUDWIG ★ ♟

Museum Ludwig is the flagship among Cologne's museums. It houses the city's entire art collection from the 20th and 21st centuries. A collector couple – Peter and Irene Ludwig – donated their collection of Pop Art to the city in 1968. Later Peter Ludwig also brought lesser-known avant-garde works from Russia to the Rhine. He remained an active collector right up to the last years of his life (he died in 1996), collecting artworks from China and Cuba that epitomised the idea of "Global Art" – an expression of shared life experiences among the younger generation of artists, whether they are from Havana, Shanghai, Berlin or New York.

This Ludwigs' collection still forms the basis of the permanent exhibition to this day. Thanks to a donation by Irene Ludwig in 2001, the museum houses the third-largest Picasso collection in the world, which you can view in splendid isolation if you get to the museum early enough. It is also worth taking a look at the Expressionists, including Ernst Ludwig Kirchner, Max Beckmann and others, as well as works from the Fluxus and Nouveau réalisme movements of the 1960s (Arman, Yves Klein, Daniel Spoerri, etc.). Temporary exhibitions are often very popular. *Tue–Sun 10am–6pm, first Thu of the month*

INSIDER TIP
Spend the morning with Pablo

until 10pm | Heinrich-Böll-Platz 1 | admission 11 euros | museum-ludwig. de | U-Bahn, S-Bahn and buses: Dom/ Hbf | ⊙ 3 hrs | ▥ c1

2 ROMAN NORTH GATE

At the northern end of the cathedral square are the remains of a gate that was part of the Roman city walls. Even 2,000 years ago it was quite draughty here, which is why local novelist Heinrich Böll once surmised that the guards must have constantly caught colds on duty. *Trankgasse/Domplatte | U-Bahn, S-Bahn and buses: Dom/Hbf | ▥ b1*

3 DOM (CATHEDRAL) ★

Twin 157m spires, a massive and imposing central structure and astonishing attention to detail all contribute to Cologne cathedral's status as a must-see building for believers and non-believers alike. The whole city identifies with its cathedral and sings its praises at full volume, at least during carnival season. The church attracts more than six million visitors each year, making it one of Germany's most-visited sights.

The cathedral owes its construction to the legends of St Gereon and St Ursula, which first established *Hillige Kölle* (Holy Cologne) as a place of pilgrimage in the early Middle Ages. In 1164, the purported remains of the Three Kings were brought to Cologne from Milan and housed in a specially made shrine. Of course, a suitably

Lights, music and heavenly architecture: a communion service in the cathedral

grandiose cathedral then had to be built around the shrine. The cornerstone was laid in 1248. Master Gerhard, the first master of works for the cathedral, favoured the high-Gothic style of contemporary French churches. However, subsequent construction was painfully slow, and it stopped entirely in 1560 due to the plague and to the city's economic decline; it wouldn't recommence for another 250 years. In fact, it was Prussian Protestants that finally completed the cathedral in 1880, at which point it was the tallest building in the world.

Inside, don't miss the modern glass window designed by local artist Gerhard Richter. The coloured glass squares are at their most beautiful in the light of the midday sun. Also notable is the figure of the "Lady of Grace" in front of the *Dreikönigenaltar* in the northern transept, and the wooden pulpit, which dates from 1544. At the end of the ambulatory is the altar dedicated to the patron saints of the city, St Ursula and St Gereon. The altarpiece was originally painted for the town hall chapel by Stefan Lochner.

INSIDER TIP
A glass mosaic

It takes about half an hour to climb the *Domturm* (cathedral tower), with its 533 steps, but it's worth it for the unparalleled view from the top *(Mar, April, Oct daily 9am–5pm; May–Sept daily 9am–6pm; Nov–Feb daily 9am–4pm | Domkloster 4 | admission 6 euros)*. The huge Peter's Bell in the belfry is called *dä decke Pitter* or "fat Peter" in Kölsch. When it was cast in Apolda in 1923, it was the largest ringable bell in the world, at 24 tons.

In 1969 a square (the *Domplatte*), designed by the architect Fritz Schaller, was laid out around the cathedral. Although the eastern and northern sides were subsequently redesigned, the square is still criticised for not being worthy of the cathedral it surrounds. At least the façade of the long-empty Dom-Hotel has now been completely renovated and is ready to welcome visitors again.

Kölner Dommusik (koelner-dom musik.de) holds ♥ free concerts in the cathedral's *Dreikönigenschrein* (Shrine of the Three Kings); also free are the organ celebrations, which take place in the cathedral at 8pm on Tuesdays from June to September. There's a collection at the end of the concert.

Cathedral Mon–Sat 6am–8pm, Sun 1–4pm | guided tours Mon–Sat 10.30am, 2pm (English) and 3pm (10 euros); rooftop tour 3pm only (20 euros) | Multivision in the Domforum Cinema (opposite the West portal): Mon–Sat 10.45am, 12.45pm, 2.45pm and 3.45pm, Sun 2.45pm and 3.45pm | admission 2 euros | koel-ner-dom.de, domforum.de | U-Bahn, S-Bahn and buses: Dom/Hbf. ⏱ *2 hrs |* 🗺 *c1*

🔲 ROMAN HARBOUR ROAD

The Roman road that leads to the Römisch-Germanischen Museum has been reconstructed using original paving stones. *Roncalliplatz | East Side | U-Bahn, S-Bahn and buses: Dom/Hbf |* 🗺 *c2*

ALTSTADT

Komödienstraße
Burgmauer
Dom (Cathedral) ★ 3 Tankgasse
Roman north gate 2
Am Domhof
1 Museum Ludwig ★
Rheinufertunnel
Heinzelmännchen-Brunnen 5 Am Hof
4 Roman harbour road
Große Neugasse
Tunisstraße
Ludwigstraße
Hohe Straße
6 Praetorium Mühlengasse
Alter Markt 12 Statue of Tünnes and Schäl
Time Ride Cologne 11 7
8 Gross St Martin 9 Fischmarkt ★
Historic Rathaus 13 U Lintgasse
Herzogstraße
Archaeological Zone/MiQua 14
10 Ostermannbrunnen
Fastnachtsbrunnen 15 16 Wallraf-Richartz Museum & Fondation Corboud ★
Buttermarkt
Nord-Süd-Faht
18 Gürzenich
Alt St Alban's 17
Heumarkt
Heumarkt
Rhine
Schildergasse
Große Sandkaul
Gürzenichstraße
Augustinerstr. U Heumarkt Deutzer Brücke
Pippinstraße
Cäcilienstraße
Heumarkt
Am Leystapel
22 Römisch-Germanisches Museum 19 St Maria im Kapitol
Sternengasse
20 Overstolzenhaus
Marienplatz
▲
200 m
219 yd
Mühlenbach
Filzgraben
21 St Maria Lyskirchen

5 HEINZELMÄNNCHEN-BRUNNEN

This fountain depicts a fairytale by August Kopisch from 1836. It describes how, during the night, hard-working elves did all the work so that the residents of Cologne could be lazy during the day. But a tailor's wife was curious and wanted to see the elves, so one night she scattered peas on her stairs. The elves slipped on the peas, tumbled downstairs and then disappeared forever. In the symbolism of the fairytale, the sleeping residents represent medieval Cologne and its centuries-old structures. It was Napoleon's occupying forces that first gave the city a modern administration in around 1800; from then on, Cologne started to become a modern city of business and economic prosperity. *Am Hof | U-Bahn, S-Bahn and buses: Dom/Hbf |* 🗺 *b–c2*

6 PRAETORIUM

The former palace complex of the Roman governor (Praetor) was first discovered in 1953 during reconstruction of the "new" city hall (also known as the *Spanische Bau* – Spanish Building). The palace included under-floor heating to ward off the cold. The development of the archaeological zone around the *Museum im Quartier (MiQua, see p. 36)* means that the Praetorium is closed until 2026. In the meantime, a few remnants of the palace can be seen in the cathedral car park and in the cellar of Weinhaus Brung. *U-Bahn, S-Bahn and buses: Dom/Hbf, Rathaus | ⏲ 45 mins | ▥ c2*

7 STATUE OF TÜNNES & SCHÄL

The shrewd peasant Tünnes and his cunning partner, Schäl, belong to Cologne's folklore, just like carnival. Originally devised as characters for the Hänneschen puppet theatre, they were recreated in bronze by the sculptor Ewald Mataré on a commission from Jupp Engels, who also funded the neighbouring Schmitz column. Tünnes' prominent nose is shiny because rubbing it is meant to bring good luck. *Brigittengässchen | U-Bahn, S-Bahn and buses: Dom/Hbf, Rathaus | ▥ c2*

8 GROSS ST MARTIN

If it weren't for Cologne's almighty cathedral, this building would be the most notable church in the city. Founded in 1172, it represents the apotheosis of Romanesque architecture. The most prominent feature is the 75m-high crossing tower, framed by four smaller round towers. Gross St Martin was largely destroyed during World War II and rebuilt under the direction of Cologne architect Joachim Schürmann. *Tue–Fri 9am–7.30pm, Sat/Sun 10am–7.30pm | Gross St Martin 9 | romanische-kirchen-koeln. de | U-Bahn, S-Bahn and buses: Dom/Hbf, Rathaus | ⏲ 45 mins | ▥ c2*

9 FISCHMARKT ★

The narrow but colourful gabled houses on the *Fischmarkt* (fish market) are one of the most photogenic images in the Altstadt. Fish (much of it from the Netherlands) was traded here from the 13th century onwards, but today the square's main attraction is its numerous beer gardens.

Between Gross St Martin and the *Rheingarten* lies the extensive *Stapelhaus* (storehouse): during the Middle Ages all ships travelling on the Rhine had to drop anchor in Cologne for three days and present their wares at the *Stapelhaus*. This gave Cologne's tradesmen control of trade on the river. *U-Bahn and buses: Heumarkt | ▥ c2*

10 OSTERMANNBRUNNEN

Willi Ostermann (1876–1936) is universally admired in Cologne. He wrote more than 100 patriotic songs and carnival hits that are an intrinsic part of the city's character. This memorial fountain (1938) shows characters from his songs. *Ostermannplatz | U-Bahn and buses: Heumarkt | ▥ c2*

11 TIME RIDE COLOGNE ☂

Take a virtual trip back in time to visit Cologne in the 1920s or to travel through 2,000 years of the city's history – all possible thanks to VR headsets. It's a great way to pass the time on a rainy day or when you're tired of tramping the 21st-century streets. *Mon 2–7pm, Tue–Sun 11am–7pm | Alter Markt 36–42 | tel. 0221 98 86 63 30 | timeride.de/koeln | U-Bahn and buses: Heumarkt |* ⏱ *50 mins | ▢ c2*

12 ALTER MARKT

The *Alter Markt* (old market) is the heart of the Altstadt. It is car-free and often bathed in sunshine. Look up towards the roof of house number 24 to spot the figure of the *Kallendresser* ("gutter-shitter") with his naked buttocks on display. From the terraces of the somewhat old-fashioned cafés, you will have a view of the historic town hall, the Jan von Werth Fountain and the Alter Markt's colourful medieval houses. Built in 1884, the fountain has a story behind it: Jan von Werth was a simple farm boy who was rejected by the maid Griet. When Jan returned from the Thirty Years' War as a proud cavalry general, Griet (now a flower-seller) regretted her decision. *U-Bahn, S-Bahn and buses: Dom/Hbf, Rathaus, Heumarkt | ▢ c2*

13 HISTORIC RATHAUS (CITY HALL)

The self-confidence of the citizens of medieval Cologne is evident in the 61m-high tower of the late-Gothic *Rathaus*, completed in 1414. It was constructed to compete visually with nearby Gross St Martin church. At the back of the building is another dramatic symbol of civic pride: the

You won't be the first to give Tünnes' nose a rub

so-called *Platzjabbeck*, a carved wooden head that sticks its tongue out every hour.

On the west side, the city hall's striking Renaissance gallery dates back to the year 1573. Archaeologists have also discovered a first-century portico at the *Rathaus* – the colonnade is decorated with round arches. At the heart of the building is the *Piazetta* (atrium), which is usually freely accessible. Note: the city hall is surrounded by a huge building site as part of the extensive excavation work for the Archaeological Zone and can only be visited on a guided tour with *Köln Tourismus (see p. 128). Rathausplatz | U-Bahn, S-Bahn and buses: Dom/Hbf, Rathaus | ⏱ 45 mins | ▥ c2*

▦ ARCHAEOLOGICAL ZONE/ MIQUA ⚑

Cologne is more than 2,000 years old, and its history is tangible in much of the city. But it would be an exaggeration to claim that the past pervades the present. That's why the creation of an *Archaeological Zone* in the historic centre of the city is a great idea. The focal point is an excavation site between the *Historic Rathaus (see p. 35)*, the new city hall (or *Spanische Bau*), the *Farina Fragrance Museum* and the *Wallraf-Richartz Museum*. Extensive excavations have been under way here, in the centre of the old Jewish quarter, since 2007. The aim is to create a 6,000m² exhibition complex, known as the "MiQua" *(Museum im Quartier)*, which will bring to life the city's 2,000-year history. It is scheduled to open in 2026. The centrepiece will be the new *Jüdisches Museum* (Jewish Museum), which will provide access to a *mikvah*, a Jewish ceremonial bath dating from the 12th century. Other historical sites will be integrated into the complex under the auspices of the Rhineland Regional Association (LVR). The fourth-century Roman governor's palace, the *Praetorium* (see p. 35), is particularly impressive; from the antechamber there's a view into the Roman sewer system. *For the latest updates, see museenkoeln.de/archaeologische-zone and miqua.blog | U-Bahn and buses:*

A moment of solitude in the Wallraf-Richartz Museum

Heumarkt, Rathaus | ⏱ *30 mins* |
🗺 *c2*

15 FASTNACHTSBRUNNEN

In 1825 Goethe participated in the carnival and then warned against its wild excesses with the words, "a little madness is commendable when it is brief and for a reason…" This inscription adorns Georg Grassegger's fountain (1913) alongside figures from Cologne's folklore: the *Rote Funken* dressed as city soldiers; the *Hillige Mägde un Knäächte* (holy maids and servants) – the oldest dance troupe in the carnival; and a figure in *Kluten* costume, the traditional dress of Rhine harbour workers. *Gülichplatz | karneval.de | U-Bahn and buses: Heumarkt | 🗺 c2*

16 WALLRAF-RICHARTZ MUSEUM & FONDATION CORBOUD ★

Housed in a modern and functional building designed by Cologne architect Oswald Mathias Ungers (1926–2007), this museum is worth a visit not least for van Gogh's *Drawbridge* painting and for the great views of the cathedral. The collection encompasses many artistic movements from the medieval period through to 19th-century Impressionism, and includes a Rembrandt self-portrait in old age from c. 1668. A crowd-pleasing highlight is the densely hung Impressionist section with works by the likes of Claude Monet and Lovis Corinth. *Tue-Sun 10am–6pm, 1st and 3rd Thu each month 10am–10pm | Obenmarspforten (Am Kölner Rathaus) | admission 13 euros, admission for special exhibitions varies | wallraf.museum | U-Bahn, S-Bahn and buses: Dom/Hbf, Heumarkt or Rathaus | 🕙 2 hrs | 🗺 c2*

INSIDER TIP
Art with a view

17 ALT ST ALBAN

Only the ruins are left of this parish church, which was destroyed in 1945. A copy of the statue of the *Mourning Parents* by Käthe Kollwitz (1931) was placed in the ruins as a memorial to those who died during World War II. *Quatermarkt 4 | U-Bahn and buses: Heumarkt | 🗺 c2*

18 GÜRZENICH

Today, the Gürzenich is mainly known for the enthronement of the carnival's Cologne triumvirate. Originally, however, it was built to honour other dignitaries. Medieval emperors were crowned 70km away in Aachen and often stopped over in Cologne. In order to receive them, an impressive ceremonial building was needed; in 1437, the council decided to build an imposing banqueting and dance hall large enough for 4,000 guests. Later on the building served as a warehouse; it wasn't until the 19th century that it was first used as a concert hall and ballroom. *Martinstr. 29–31/ Quatermarkt | U-Bahn and buses: Heumarkt | f c2*

19 ST MARIA IM KAPITOL

Do you need a break from the city? Then visit this wonderful Romanesque church and enjoy a moment's peace in the magical rose garden in the cloisters.

INSIDER TIP
Take time out

The church building, consecrated in 1065, is considered unique because of its triconchos choir and its mixture of a central plan and nave basilica structure. *Mon–Sat 10am–6pm, Sun 1–6pm | Kasinostr. 6 | romanische-kirchen-koeln.de | U-Bahn and buses: Heumarkt | ⟳ 1 hr | ▥ c3*

20 OVERSTOLZENHAUS

Now the site of the Academy for Media, this is the oldest domestic house still in use in the city. It was built in 1230 by the Overstolz family, who were wealthy wine merchants. With its stepped gables, it is the only remaining patrician house in the Romanesque style. *Rheingasse 8 | U-Bahn and buses: Heumarkt | ▥ c3*

21 ST MARIA LYSKIRCHEN

A mark on the exterior, high above the entrance, indicates the record high-water mark reached in 1784. It's also worth stepping inside this church, which was first mentioned in a document in 984, in order to see the beautiful, vaulted ceiling and the murals of biblical scenes. Often, you'll have the church to yourself. *Mon–Sat 10am–6pm, Sun 10am–4pm | An Lyskirchen 8 | romanische-kirchen-koeln.de | U-Bahn and buses: Heumarkt | ⟳ 30 mins | ▥ c3*

22 RÖMISCH-GERMANISCHES MUSEUM

The Roman-Germanic museum is shut for major renovation work until late 2024/early 2025; for up-to-date information, consult the website. In the meantime, a selection of the most important exhibits are on display in the much smaller *Belgisches Haus*. The unique collection consists of archaeological finds from Cologne's earliest period as a Roman settlement. *Wed–Mon 10am–6pm | Belgisches Haus | Cäcilienstrasse 46 | admission 6 euros | museenkoeln.de | U-Bahn and buses: Neumarkt | ⟳ 2 hrs | ▥ a3*

CITY CENTRE

Even now, the elderly residents of outlying suburbs such as Nippes and Ehrenfeld will say, "I am going into town," when they go shopping in the city centre.

Shop till you drop on Schildergasse

"Centre" here means the medieval part of Cologne between the Rhine and the *Ring* boulevard. The district is divided in a cross shape by two axes: the Roman military road from Bonn to Neuss runs north to south between the Eigelstein and Severin city gates, while Hahnenstrasse, Neumarkt and Schildergasse form the east–west axis. During the Middle Ages, Schildergasse was home to the city's signwriters (*Schild* = sign).

23 KULTURZENTRUM NEUMARKT ☔

Anyone interested in the cultural variety of our planet should pay this centre a visit. Opened in 2010, the centre combines the Rautenstrauch-Joest Museum of world cultures with the Schnütgen Museum for sacred art.

Visitors to the *Rautenstrauch-Joest Museum* are greeted by a 7m-high Indonesian rice barn, which dominates the entrance hall. Other exhibits are arranged according to 12 themes, including "Home life", "Religion" and "Stereotypes and prejudice".

A glass-covered passage connects the main building to the *Schnütgen Museum* in neighbouring St Cecilia church. Here, the collection of religious art includes wonderful wood and stone sculptures, precious medieval carved altarpieces, chasubles, textiles, fine gold, silver and bronze metalwork, ivory carvings, stained-glass windows, Roman and Gothic sculptures, reverse glass paintings and large items of church furniture. *Tue–Sun 10am–6pm, Thu 10am–8pm, until 10pm on the 1st Thu of the* month | Cäcilienstr. 29–33 | admission: Rautenstrauch-Joest Museum 7 euros, Schnütgen Museum 6 euros, combined ticket 10 euros | museenkoeln. de | U-Bahn and buses: Neumarkt | ⏱ 2 hrs | 🗺 a3

24 KOLUMBA ★

The museum of the Cologne archdiocese is best known for its architecture: Swiss architect Peter Zumthor's spectacular building successfully integrates its Roman and Gothic predecessors. It includes a confessional chapel, which is one of the most popular places of worship in the city. The chapel was constructed by master-builder Gottfried Böhm (1920–2021) after World War II. Böhm remains the only German recipient of the internationally renowned Pritzker Prize for architecture. The museum itself shows far more than just sacred art and covers all artistic eras from antiquity to the present day. Exhibits are regularly rotated and refreshed. Wed–Mon noon–5pm | Kolumbastr. 2–4 | admission 8 euros | kolumba.de | U-Bahn, S-Bahn and buses: Dom/Hbf | 🗺 b2

INSIDER TIP
A place of peace

25 KÖLNISCHES STADTMUSEUM

What did people like to do in the Middle Ages; what about 200 years ago or 50 years ago? What do the people of Cologne believe in, and what do they want? This relocated museum uses questions like these to illuminate 2,000 years of city history. Particularly innovative is the "Cologne in 20 Minutes" exhibit, which includes a model of the city in 1571. For opening times, see website | Minoritenstr. 11 | koelnisches-stadtmuseum.de | U-Bahn and buses: Appellhofplatz | ⏱ 1 hr | 🗺 b2

26 MUSEUM FÜR ANGEWANDTE KUNST

The well-presented collection demonstrates how applied art and design have influenced how we live since the Middle Ages. The permanent exhibition showcases, among many other things, art-nouveau porcelain, wedding garments from the 1930s, as well as furniture, pewter and television sets. There are also worthwhile special exhibitions on pop-cultural themes. There's a peaceful café in the interior courtyard. Tue–Sun 10am–6pm, until 10pm on 1st Thu of each month | An der Rechtschule | admission 4 euros, or 9 euros with special exhibition | makk. de | U-Bahn, S-Bahn and buses: Dom/Hbf | ⏱ 2 hrs | 🗺 b2

INSIDER TIP
Coffee break

27 ST ANDREAS

Post-World War II urban planners did not take much care when they reconstructed the area around the station, which means this 13th-century Romanesque church gets rather lost among the brutalist architecture. But the new windows attract attention, as they were designed by the eccentric modern artist Markus Lüpertz. Parts of the crypt date from the 11th century. They house a sarcophagus with the remains of St Albertus Magnus. Mon–Fri 7.30am–6pm, Sat/Sun 8am–6pm |

CITY CENTRE

St Gereon **34**

Gereonstraße

Unt. Sachsenhausen

Im Klapperhof

Mohenstr.

Komödienstraße **27** St Andreas

Zeughaus **29** **28** Roman fountain

Burgmauer

Friesenviertel

33 **32** Friesenstrasse **31** Roman tower

30 El-De Haus

Magnusstraße

Albertusstraße

Tunisstraße

26 Museum für Angewandte Kunst

Kölnisches Stadtmuseum **25**

24 Kolumba ★

Hohenzollernring

Friesenwall

Alte Wallg.

Breite Straße

Krebsgasse

Glockengasse

Ludwigstraße

Marsplfortengasse

35 Ehrenstrasse

Pfeilstraße

Richmodstraße

36 Hahnentor

Kölnischer Kunstverein

37

38 St Aposteln

Schildergasse

Nord-

Hahnenstraße

Neumarkt

Am Rinkenpfuhl

Marsilstein

23 Cäcilienstraße Kulturzentrum Neumarkt

Süd-Fahrt

Sternengasse

Hohenstaufenring

Rubensstraße

Clemensstr.

Thieboldsgasse

Fleischmengergasse

Agrippastraße

Mauritiuswall

Mauritiussteinweg

Kleiner Griechenmarkt

Blaubach

Huhnsgasse

Rothgerberbach

Perlengraben

200 m
217 yd

39 St Pantaleon

Komödienstr. 4–8 | *romanische-kirchen-koeln.de* | U-Bahn, S-Bahn and buses: Dom/ Hbf | ⏱ 30 mins | 🗺 b1

28 ROMAN FOUNTAIN

Franz Brantzky created this fountain in 1915. It depicts scenes from Roman history on relief panels, and the legend of the she-wolf who

suckled Romulus and Remus is shown on a column. *Between Burgmauer and Komödienstr.* | *U-Bahn and buses: Appellhofplatz* | 🗺 b1

29 ZEUGHAUS

Until 2017, the Kölnisches Stadt-museum (see p. 40) was housed in this historic armoury building, but it

The impressive Romanesque church of St Gereon incorporates some Roman stonework

was forced to move due to water damage. The future of the *Zeughaus*, built in 1600, remains unclear. *Minoritenstr. 13 | U-Bahn and buses: Appellhofplatz | ▥ a1*

⒊⒋ EL-DE HAUS

This cellar with its prison cells is a reminder of terrible times: during the Nazi era, the Gestapo tortured prisoners here. Inscriptions on the walls document the prisoners' suffering. There are regular special exhibitions on the topic of Cologne under the Nazis. *Tue–Fri 10am–6pm, Sat/Sun 11am–6pm, until 10pm on 1st Thu of the month | Appellhofplatz 23–25 | admission 4.50 euros, for details of tours (groups only), see website, booking essential, tel. 0221 22 12 63 31 | museenkoeln.de/ns-dokumenta tionszentrum | U-Bahn and buses: Appellhofplatz | ⏱ 1½ hrs | ▥ a1–2*

⒊⒈ ROMAN TOWER

Dating back to 50 CE, the corner tower of the Roman city wall, with its natural-stone mosaic, is a bit lost in modern-day Cologne, but it's still worth a look. *St-Apern-Str./Zeughausstr. | U-Bahn and buses: Appellhofplatz | ▥ a1*

⒊⒉ FRIESENSTRASSE

At the weekend, tourists from the countryside flock to old favourites here, such as *Klein Köln*, but there are also plenty of new cocktail bars, hip restaurants, food kiosks and a

34 ST GEREON

Many Cologne residents are indifferent to their surroundings, but the Romanesque churches in the city are a unique cultural asset. A good example is the impressive 12th-century church of St Gereon, with its floor mosaics. *Daily 9am–6pm | Gereonsdriesch 4 | romanische-kirchen-koeln.de | U-Bahn 12, 15 Christophstrasse/Mediapark | ⏱ 30 mins | ▥ a1*

35 EHRENSTRASSE

Even though its small, quirky boutiques have largely given way to large chain stores, Ehrenstrasse remains the city's favourite shopping street. After all, fashionistas know that the fashion chains on this street only have branches in a few select cities, so they come here to see and be seen, especially on Saturdays. Ehrenstrasse had a boost in 2022, when it was transformed into a pedestrian-only zone. *U-Bahn and buses: Neumarkt, Rudolfplatz, Friesenplatz | ▥ E–F5*

36 HAHNENTOR

Along with the Eigelsteintor and Severinstor, the Hahnentor – a typical double tower gate – is one of three remaining medieval city gates. Fortunately, an obsolete pedestrian bridge and dilapidated office block on Rudolfplatz have now been demolished, but there remains a modern extension on the east façade of the tower that looks completely out of place. *Rudolfplatz/An d'r Hahnepooz | U-Bahn and buses: Rudolfplatz | ▥ E5*

brewhouse to discover. Sometimes the street is so full of people that cars can't get through! *U-Bahn and buses: Friesenplatz | ▥ E4*

33 FRIESENVIERTEL

The corporate base of the Gerling insurance group was built here between 1945 and 1953. After that, it became an exclusive residential and business district. Thanks to the opening of the hip *25 Hours Hotel*, with its *Monkey Bar and Restaurant Nemi*, the area increasingly attracts Cologne residents, who drift over from the cocktail bars, hip restaurants and sushi joints on *Friesenstrasse* (see p.42). *U-Bahn and buses: Friesenplatz | ▥ E4*

37 KÖLNISCHER KUNSTVEREIN

The city's art association tends to exhibit experimental art installations by young artists. Supplementary film programmes are also often shown in its cinema. *Tue–Sun 11am–6pm | Hahnenstr. 6 | admission 4 euros | tel. 0221 21 70 21 | koelnischerkunst verein.de | U-Bahn and buses: Neumarkt | ⏱ 1 hr | ◫ E5*

38 ST APOSTELN

Everyone always goes on about Cologne's cathedral, but this High Romanesque church, dating from about 1030, is hardly less impressive. Boasting a 66m-high tower, it still seems to meet the aesthetic demands of visitors nearly 1,000 years later. A chapel was added in 1956 with windows decorated by the sculptor Ludwig Gies, who also designed the famous *Bundesadler* sculpture for the Bonn Bundestag. The *Adenauer Memorial* is located on the northern side of the church. Konrad Adenauer was Cologne's Lord Mayor from 1917 to 1933 and again for a few months during 1945, before becoming the first Chancellor of West Germany in 1949. *Daily 10am–1pm and 2–5pm | Apostelnkloster 10 | romanische-kirchen-koeln.de | U-Bahn and buses: Neumarkt | ⏱ 30 mins | ◫ a2*

39 ST PANTALEON

The oldest Romanesque church in the city is tucked away in a tourist no-man's land. But it's worth finding: the 11th-century structure, with its round towers, is enchanting. When the church is lit up at night, the surrounding park, dotted with a few benches, becomes one of the prettiest places in the city.

INSIDER TIP
Romanesque romance

Mon–Fri 9am–noon and 12.45–5pm, Sat 9am–5pm, Sun 12.30–5pm | Am Pantaleonsberg 12 | romanische-kirchen-koeln.de | U-Bahn and buses: Poststrasse | ⏱ 30 mins | ◫ a4

DEUTZ

On the opposite side of the Rhine from the city centre, the district of Deutz encompasses several important urban facilities, including the Kölnmesse trade fair site the Lanxess Arena, the city administration and the Triangle building, along with a newly constructed boulevard along the river.

Yet the residents of Cologne still refer to the east bank as the "wrong side" of the river – *Schäl Sick* in Kölsch. Nevertheless, it is the Deutz side that affords the best view of the cathedral and the Altstadt. In 310, the Romans installed a wooden pontoon bridge where the Deutzer Bridge is today. The crossing was protected by the Divitia fort on the right bank of the Rhine. However, given the large number of Roman relics in the city, this site has never been regarded as worthy of excavation.

40 RHEINBOULEVARD

Since major renovations in 2016, the riverbank in Deutz has boasted an attractive boulevard between the

Rheinpark and the Poller Wiesen. First, take a stroll along the river, then have a seat on the steps of the ★ *Rheintreppe* and enjoy the unsurpassed view of the cathedral, river and Altstadt. Refreshment is provided by two bars in the Hyatt Hotel. *Kennedy-Ufer | trains and buses: Deutz/Messe | 🗺 d2*

41 KÖLN TRIANGLE 👓

Getting up to the 28th floor by elevator only takes half a minute! Then a further 29 steps take you up to the viewing platform at 103m. On a clear day there are breathtaking views of the city as well as the distant hills. *Daily 11am–8pm | Ottoplatz 1 | admission 5 euros | koelntrianglepanorama. de | trains and buses: Deutz/Messe | 🗺 H4*

42 LANXESS ARENA

Germany's largest indoor arena for sporting events, shows, parties and concerts offers space for a total of 20,000 spectators. It is the home stadium for the Cologne Sharks ice-hockey team. *Willy-Brandt-Platz 3 | Ticket hotline tel. 0221 80 20 | lanxess-arena.de | U-Bahn and buses: Deutz/ Kölnarena | 🗺 J5*

43 KM 689 COLOGNE BEACH CLUB

In the words of the Kölsch band Paveier, this is "the only beach with a view of the Dom". Relax on the soft sand below the dancing fountain and you'll feel as though you really are at the seaside. *May–Sept Fri–Sun from noon and for events | Rheinpark | admission free | km689.rhein-terrassen.de | trains and buses: Deutz/Messe | 🗺 H4*

Take a seat on the Rheintreppe – the perfect place to spend a summer evening

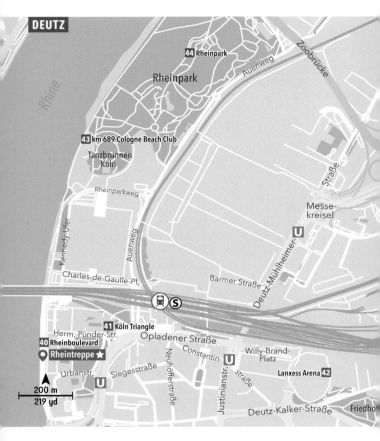

44 RHEINPARK 🛶 🎭

Rheinpark was created and opened for the 1957 German Garden Show. The park has large flower beds and is packed with people on sunny days. Children have fun on the narrow-gauge railway, while adults appreciate the benefits of the ☂ Claudius thermal baths whose water is a soothing 30°C.

From here you can take a thrilling but comfortable trip to the zoo by 🎭 cable car across the Rhine (mid-Mar–early Nov daily 10am–6pm | from 5 euros | koelner-seilbahn.de | Trains and buses: Deutz/Messe | ⌖ H3–4

INSIDER TIP
High above the river

EIGELSTEIN DISTRICT

Kölsch and kebabs, pubs and gourmet restaurants, brewhouses and bistros: all thrive side by side in this district.

The rather bleak areas around the railway embankment are sometimes used as filming locations for the popular German TV crime series *Tatort*.

45 EIGELSTEINTORBURG

When Napoleon conquered Cologne, he took the opportunity to enter through the Eigelsteintorburg. That is just one of many episodes in the rich history of the city gate, which was originally called the *Adlerpforte*. During the French occupation (1794–1814) it was renamed the *Porte d'Aigle*, which was then Germanised as *Eigel*. Those citizens who donated their wedding rings to be melted down during World War I were allowed to hammer a nail into the statue of the *Kölsche Boor* (Cologne farmer), which represented the valour of the city. A relief of this medieval farmer can be seen on the left tower. The inscription indicates that the statue was later reinterpreted as a symbol of loyalty towards the Empire. It loosely translates as, "Hold on to the Kingdom, farmer. Let it not fall, be the times sweet or sour". *Eigelstein | U-Bahn and buses: Ebertplatz | ▥ G3*

46 STAVENHOF

This little alley used to be the city's most notorious den of sin. But where prostitution and crime long held sway, you'll now find one of the city's few picturesque streets – it's particularly beautiful in the soft light at dusk. *Im Stavenhof | U-Bahn and buses: Ebertplatz, S-Bahn: Hansaring | ▥ F3*

INSIDER TIP
Change of scene

47 WEIDENGASSE

If you like variety, head for the Weidengasse, where Cologne junk shops and Turkish lamb butchers sit side by side. A good example of socio-cultural transformation and urban renewal is the old scissor sharpener's shop that now sells expensive gourmet kitchen knives. *U-Bahn and buses: Ebertplatz | ▥ F3*

Lanxess Arena

EIGELSTEIN DISTRICT

48 GEREONSMÜHLENTURM

An original piece of the medieval city wall stands in this section of the Gereonswall. Today, the mill tower is used as a venue for parties. *Gereonswall | U-Bahn, S-Bahn and buses: Hansaring | 🗺 F4*

49 ST URSULA ★

The Cologne coat of arms is decorated with 11 black flames, which represent the British princess Ursula and her following of 11,000 maidens. According to legend, they were all massacred when the Huns besieged Cologne. The remains of Holy St Ursula and other relics are kept in the Golden Chamber. *Church and Golden Chamber: Tue–Sat 10am–noon and 3–5pm | Ursulaplatz 30 | romanische-kirchen-koeln.de | U-Bahn, S-Bahn and buses: Dom/Hbf | ⏱ 30 mins | 🗺 F4*

50 ST KUNIBERT

This massive sacred building, clearly visible from the opposite bank of the Rhine in Deutz, was consecrated in 1247 and is the last city church of the Romanesque era. *Daily 10am–6pm | Kunibertskloster 6 | romanische-kirchen-koeln.de | U-Bahn and buses: Breslauer Platz | ⏱ 30 mins | ▥ G4*

51 WECKSCHNAPP

During the Middle Ages this little tower served as a prison. When the inmates were desperate for something to eat, they had to grab *(Schnapp)* for a piece of bread *(Weck)* that was dangled down to them on a string. *Konrad-Adenauer-Ufer 73 | weckschnapp.de | U-Bahn and buses: Ebertplatz | ▥ G3*

SEVERINS DISTRICT/ SÜDSTADT

The Südstadt is a vibrant district, set apart from the downtown area in the south of the city. In many streets, the turn-of-the-century buildings remain largely intact. Despite increasing gentrification, the population is refreshingly diverse: aging ex-squatters, eco-conscious academics, artists, local blue-collar workers and Turkish greengrocers.

This is an area of the city that is filled with history: the pub *Früh em Veedel*, for example, is known locally as the "cathedral of the invalids" because veterans from World War I used to meet here. For an authentic street carnival experience, spend Weiberfastnacht (Thursday before Ash Wednesday) at An der Eiche or Severinskirchplatz *(▥ G7)*.

**INSIDER TIP
Traditional fun**

52 SCHOKOLADENMUSEUM 🏆

A greenhouse for cocoa, a never-ending chocolate fountain, all kinds of equipment for chocolate production and refinement – and, of course, a tasting room, where chocolate-making courses are held. These features have made the Chocolate Museum (now part of the Lindt Group) one of the city's most popular attractions. Climb the outside steps to the roof for a panoramic view of the Rhine, the cathedral and the Old Town. *Daily 10am–6pm | Rheinauhafen 1a | admission 13.50 euros | schokoladenmuseum.de | U-Bahn: Heumarkt or Severinstrasse, Bus 106 Schokoladenmuseum | ⏱ 2 hrs | ▥ c–d 3–4*

**INSIDER TIP
A sweet view**

53 DEUTSCHES SPORT & OLYMPIAMUSEUM

An entertaining exhibition chronicling the history of German Olympians and other sports stars. Exhibits include the tennis raquet that Boris Becker destroyed and shoes belonging to Formula One World Champion Michael Schumacher. You can also test your own sporting skills: throw punches at a punch bag, ride a bicycle

INSIDER TIP
Kick it sky high

in a wind tunnel or head to the roof to kick a ball around on the city's highest football pitch. *Tue–Sun 10am–6pm | Rheinauhafen 1 | admission 9.50 euros | group tours tel. 0221 33 60 90 | sportmuseum.info | U-Bahn and buses: Heumarkt or Severinstrasse | ⏱ 1½ hrs | ▥ c–d4*

☷ RHEINAUHAFEN ★

Only a tiny yacht harbour remains of what was once a Prussian excise port. The area is now characterised by modern buildings, museums, galleries and other businesses unrelated to its

The Rheinauhafen has become one of the city's top destinations

maritime past. The beer garden at *Hafenterrasse am Malakoffturm* (1855) has a beautiful view of the old swing bridge and the Chocolate Museum. *Holzmarkt | buses 132, 133; U-Bahn: Severinstrasse | ▥ c4*

☷ BAYENTURM

This tower was the southern outpost of the medieval city wall which was built in a semicircle as far as the *Weckschnapp (see p. 49)* in the north. Today this building is used as a media, information and documentation centre for the history of women's emancipation and serves as the editorial office for the feminist magazine, *Emma*. *Mon–Fri 10am–5pm, tours on the last Wed of the month, 5 euros, enquire online | Am Bayenturm | frauenmediaturm.de | U-Bahn: Ubierring | ▥ G7*

☷ SEVERINSTORBURG

Just like the *Eigelsteintorburg (see p. 47)*, the *Severinstorburg* is a physical reminder of Cologne's history. Sited at the end of the wonderfully varied Severinstrasse, this fortified gatehouse is a notable landmark and a popular venue for weddings. Vines are grown in the tiny garden. On *Weiberfastnacht (the Thursday before Ash Wednesday), Dat Spill vun Jan un Griet* – a play about the Cavalry General Jan von Werth – is performed here. *Chlodwigplatz 2 | U-Bahn and buses: Chlodwigplatz | ▥ G7*

☷ ST SEVERIN

The building of a first church on this site during the fourth century is

SEVERINS DISTRICT/SÜDSTADT

Große Witschgasse
52 Schokoladenmuseum
Rheinauhafen ★ 54
Rheinaustraße
53 Deutsches Sport & Olympiamuseum
Blaubach
Tel-Aviv-Straße
Severinstraße
Im Sionstal
Holzmarkt
Severinsbrücke
Perlengraben
Poller
Auf der Hanseweft
Wie
Ankerstraße
Schnurgasse
Landsbergstraße
Rosenstraße
Rhine
Josephstraße
Achterstraße
Biberstraße
Bayenstraße
Ulrichgasse
Kartäusergasse
Annostraße
Dreikönigenstraße
58 Ulrepforte
Kartäuserhof
Severinstraße
57 St Severin
Bayenturm 55
Sachsen-ring
Kartäuserwall
Lothringer Straße
Severins-wall
56 Severinstorburg
Ubierring
Karolingerring
Altenburger Straße
Mainzer Straße
Trajanstraße
Agrippinaufer
Metzer Straße
Merowingerstraße
Bonner Straße
Römerpark
Katharina-Schauberg-Promenade
Rolandstraße
Teutoburger Straße

▲
200 m
219 yd

ascribed to St Severin, the third bishop of Cologne. The extensions of 948 were redesigned during the 14th and 15th centuries. *Mon–Fri 10am–6pm, Sat 10am–1pm, Sun 1–5pm | Im Ferkulum 29 | romanische-kirchen-koeln.de | U-Bahn and buses: Chlodwigplatz* ▥ *G7*

58 ULREPFORTE

A rare section of the original medieval city wall is still intact here. The *Ulrepforte* and the neighbouring *Sachsenturm* are used today as the seat of several carnival associations. On the wall is a relief panel dating from 1360, considered to be the oldest secular monument in Germany.

Ehrenfeld is not just a party district; it's also home to Germany's largest mosque

The inscription recalls the city's defence against an attack in 1268 by the Archbishop on Cologne's civilians. *Sachsenring | U-Bahn and buses: Ulrepforte* 🗺 *F7*

OTHER SIGHTS

🟥 FLORA & BOTANISCHER GARTEN 🐾

Today, only the façade remains of the venerable Flora ballroom. Behind it is a modern function room, but in front of it there is still an ornate fountain surrounded by photogenic flowerbeds. Elsewhere, the botanic garden has four fully renovated tropical greenhouses, artificial lakes and beds where indigenous plants are cultivated. *Café Dank Augusta* treats its customers to picnic-style delicacies in fine weather. *Garden: 8am–dusk | Amsterdamer Str. 34 | admission free | short.travel/ koe5 | bus: 134, U-Bahn: 15, 16 Zoo/ Flora | ⏲ 2 hrs | Riehl | 🗺 H1–2*

🟥 ZOOLOGISCHER GARTEN 🐵

About 7,000 animals are kept at Cologne Zoo. Top attractions include the *Regenwaldhaus* (rainforest house), the large enclosure for Thai elephants and the *Hippodom*, which houses hippos and crocodiles. *Summer daily 9am–6pm; winter daily 9am–5pm | Riehler Str. 173 | admission 23 euros, children 11 euros | koelnerzoo.de | bus: 135 , U-Bahn: U 15, 16 Zoo/Flora | ⏲ 3 hrs | Riehl | 🗺 H–J 1–2*

61 SKULPTURENPARK 🐾

Every two years, the roughly 30 sculptures by contemporary artists, such as Tony Cragg, Louise Bourgeois, Martin Kippenberger, Martin Willing and Markus Lüpertz are rearranged into a new formation. A successful mixture of abstract and figurative work. *April–Sept 10.30am–7pm, Oct–March 10.30am–5pm | Riehler Str., near Zoo Bridge | admission free | skulpturenparkkoeln.de | bus 135, U-Bahn: U 15, 16 Zoo/Flora⏱ 45 mins |Agnesviertel | ▯▯ H2*

62 PHOTOGRAPHISCHE SAMMLUNG DER SK STIFTUNG KULTUR

This photographic collection is a hidden gem in the media park. Cologne photographer August Sander is considered a trailblazer in the history of modern photographic art. His work from the 1920s and 30s documents people in their social environments. The archive also encompasses work by other important photographers. The same building houses the *Deutsche Tanzmuseum Köln* (German Dance Museum Cologne), which chronicles the history of dance performance through posters, prints and photos. *Thu–Tue 2–7pm | Im Mediapark 7 | admission 6.50 euros (free admission on the 1st Mon of month), combined ticket with Tanzmuseum 8 euros (free admission to Tanzmuseum every Mon) | sk-kultur.de | U-Bahn: 12, 15 Christophstrasse/Mediapark |⏱ 1 hr | Neustadt-Nord | ▯▯ E3*

INSIDER TIP Avant-garde photography

63 EHRENFELD ⭐

Ehrenfeld is the vibrant home of artists and designers and also the preferred destination for party people who descend on the area from all points of the compass from Thursday to Saturday. You'll find cool clothes, art and kitsch on *Körnerstrasse*, in shops such as *Tutu et Tata (No. 15)* and *Kitsch deluxe (No. 26). Café Sehnsucht (No. 67)* serves organic produce and health foods. Start your evening in the gin and cocktail bar, *The Bär (Thebäerstr. 10 | baehrenfeld.de | U-Bahn: 3, 4 Körnerstrasse)* or the Braustelle (Christianstr. 2 | braustelle.com | U-Bahn: 3, 4 Körnerstrasse), which prides itself on selling its own-brewed Düsseldorf-style Altbier. The symbol of Ehrenfeld is Germany's largest *mosque (Venloer Str./Innere Kanalstr.),* designed by architect Paul Böhm. Another landmark is the *Heliosturm (Heliosstr.),* a lighthouse 300km from the North Sea. It was constructed to test the range of the electric lights manufactured by the former company Helios AG. *▯▯ C–D 3–4*

INSIDER TIP Düsseldorf drink

64 RING

After the demolition of the medieval fortifications, the city authorities constructed a new semicircular boulevard around the inner city, modelled on Vienna's *Ringstrasse*. The spacious area between Gereonshof and Christophstrasse is a popular place for a stroll. At the weekend, it becomes a party and cruising destination for sub-urbanites, and a police presence is

Bars on the Ring draw in the punters day and night

very much in evidence. *U-Bahn and buses: Friesenplatz, Rudolfplatz | Zentrum | ▢ E4–5*

65 BELGIAN QUARTER ★
From 1881, when the city was no longer contained by a wall, it quickly began to spread outwards, and a "new town" developed outside the *Ring*. In the 1980s, the area between Venloer Strasse and Aachener Strasse became a fashionable district with independent shops, cool bars and innovative restaurants. In fact, these characteristics also apply to the area further south as far as Luxemburger Strasse, although some locals refer to it as the *Kwartier Latäng* (Latin Quarter). *U-Bahn and buses: Friesenplatz, Rudolfplatz | ▢ D–E 4–5*

66 MUSEUM FÜR OSTASIATISCHE KUNST
The attractive cafeteria at the Museum of East Asian Art is a great place to start your visit, as its terrace offers an impressive view of the Japanese sculptor Masayuki Nagare's stone creation *Kaze no Hata* (Flag in the Wind). Inside this unique museum you will find treasures from throughout the Far East – such as valuable Chinese religious sculptures, Korean ceramics and Japanese priest figurines made from cypress wood. The *Guardian of the World* figure, which dates from the Han Dynasty (12th century), is one of the few surviving examples of its kind. *Tue–Sun 11am–5pm, until 10pm on 1st Thu of month | Universitätsstr. 100 | admission to the permanent collection 9.50 euros | museenkoeln.de | Buses 137, 961, 962, 963, 970, U-Bahn 1, 2 Universitätsstrasse/Aachener Weiher | ⏱ 1½ hrs | Belgisches Viertel | ▢ D5*

67 FRIEDHOF MELATEN
This cemetery manages to be morbid and captivating at the same time. In

the past, non-Catholics and those who died of disease (or malady – hence *Melaten*) were buried outside the city. After 1810, Melaten became the main cemetery and the final resting place for many of Cologne's famous citizens. The beautiful tombs and graves from the 19th century are worth a visit. *Nov–Feb 8am–5pm; March 8am–6pm; April–Sept 7am–8pm; Oct 8am–7pm | Aachener Str. 204 | bus 963, U-Bahn 1, 2 Melaten | between Lindenthal and Ehrenfeld | ▭ C4–5*

68 LINDENTHALER CANALS

Just a few steps away from the green belt is an unknown side of Cologne: the *Clarenbach Canal* and the *Rautenstrauch Canal* flow for about 1,200m under old chestnut trees through this chic part of town, which is largely undisturbed by traffic. You can continue your walk in the adjoining *Wildgehege im Stadtwald (see below)*. *Clarenbachkanal, Rautenstrauchkanal | between Universitätsstr., Aachener Str. and Stadtwaldgürtel | U-Bahn and buses: Melaten, Universitätsstrasse | Lindenthal | ▭ B–C5*

69 INNERER GRÜNGÜRTEL ★

The medieval layout of Cologne, originally ringed by a fortified wall, left no room for green spaces within the city. This changed at the end of the World War I, when a green belt was laid out around the city in order to provide healthy leisure opportunities for the growing urban population. The green belt stretches for 7km, from the banks of the Rhine in Riehl as far as Luxemburger Strasse, filling the space

between the railway embankment and Innere Kanalstrasse at a width of around 400m. Perfect for jogging and sunbathing, it's also popular with students for parties and barbecues, especially around the pond known as the *Aachener Weihe*. It's a wonderful institution that, unfortunately, is broken up by numerous exit roads from the city centre, and so far, the city authorities have failed to build the necessary bridges or tunnels for pedestrians and cyclists. *U-Bahn and buses: Universitätsstr., Moltkestr. | koelner-gruen.de | Zentrum | ▭ D–E 3–6*

70 WILDGEHEGE IM STADTWALD 😎

Peacocks, deer, geese, goats and other animals roam free in this forested park. During the summer pony rides are offered from the eastern entrance. *Daily 9am–dusk | Kitschburger Str. | U-Bahn: 13 Dürener Str./Gürtel | between Lindenthal and Müngersdorf | ▭ A6*

71 ODYSSEUM 😎

The Odysseum opened as an "interactive research adventure" for all ages, but it didn't prove popular enough, so the business owners came up with another idea. Since then, it has hosted blockbuster exhibitions on popular science topics, such as "Jurassic World – The Exhibition". The "Museum with the Mouse", based on a German TV programme, remains from the original concept and is aimed at children between the ages of 5 and 10. *Tue–Fri 10am–6pm, Sat/Sun and local holidays*

10am–8pm | Corintostr. 1 | admission from 29.50 euros, children (4–17) 23.50 euros (Museum with the Mouse 4.90/3 euros) | odysseum.de | S-Bahn: 12, 13 Trimbornstrasse, U-Bahn: 1, 9 Kalk-Post | ⏱ 1½ hrs | Kalk | ▯ K4

72 POLLER WIESEN 👥

The view from these meadows of the river, the Rheinauhafen and the historic centre is breathtaking. The meadows are enormous, providing enough space for football players and sun worshippers alike. They're also the perfect place for families to escape the hustle and bustle of the city. North and south of the Südbrücke | U-Bahn and buses: Poll, Raiffeisenstr. or Schönhauser Str. in Deutz | Deutz/Poll | ▯ H7–8

73 RODENKIRCHEN

This district is a favourite excursion destination thanks to its picturesque chapel, café terraces, houseboat restaurants, river beach and promenade. The boat trip from the Konrad-Adenauer-Ufer takes 65 minutes; breaks are possible. Tickets 13.50 euros | rodenkirchen.de | U-Bahn: 16 Rodenkirchen | Rodenkirchen | ▯ b7

AROUND COLOGNE

74 KÖNIGSWINTER

45km/40 mins by train

The romantic Rhine: a train journey of half an hour takes you to Königswinter, which sits on the river at the foot of the Siebengebirge ("Seven Mountains"). From here, kids can go up the steep path on a donkey to the Drachenfels, a rocky outcrop and ruined castle. If the ascent is too strenuous, take the Drachenfelsbahn, one of the oldest cog railways in Germany (12 euros return). From the summit you have fantastic views over the Rhine valley. koenigswinter.de | train Cologne–Königswinter 8.80 euros | ▯ 0

INSIDER TIP
Ride to the top

75 MAX ERNST MUSEUM BRÜHL

15km/15 mins by train

The museum has a large collection of prints and sculptures by the surrealist Max Ernst (1891–1976), who came from Brühl and found success as a painter, sculptor, draftsman and poet. As well as the permanent collection, the changing temporary exhibitions, featuring the work of (for example) David Lynch, Tim Burton or Max Beckman, are always worth a look. Tue–Sun 11am–6pm | Comesstr. 42 | admission 11 euros | tel. 0223 49 92 15 55 | maxernstmuseum.lvr.de | train: Brühl station | ⏱ 1½ hrs | ▯ a8

76 PHANTASIALAND BRÜHL 👥

25km/30 mins by car

This theme park is one of the largest and best in Europe with new attractions added every year. Daily April–June and Sept–mid-Nov 9am–6pm; July/Aug 9am–8pm; mid-Nov–mid-Jan "Winter Dream" 11am–8pm | Berggeiststr. 31–41 |

Pomp and splendour from top to bottom at Schloss Augustusburg

Brühl | admission 49.50 euros, children (4–11) 39.50 euros, special offers available online | phantasialand.de | ⏱ 4 hrs | 🗺 0

🔟 SCHLOSS AUGUSTUSBURG

15km/15 mins by train

Rhineland Prince Clemens August was following the architectural example of the French King Louis XIV when he had his old, moated castle transformed into a magnificent summer palace in the French style. The Baroque staircase by Balthasar Neumann is a highlight. A 30-minute walk along the beautiful avenue of linden trees will bring you to *Jagdschloss Falkenlust*, a hunting lodge where the prince met his mistresses. *Feb–Nov Mon-Fri 9am–4pm, Sat/Sun 10am–5pm | Schlossstr. 6 | Brühl | admission (incl. guided tour) main palace 9.50 euros, Falkenlust 7 euros, combined tour of both buildings 15 euros | schlossbruehl.de | train to Brühl station or U-Bahn 18 to Brühl-Mitte, then 10-min walk; by car via the B 51 Brühler Str./ Brühler Landstr., then follow signs for "Parkplätze" (parking) | 🗺 a8*

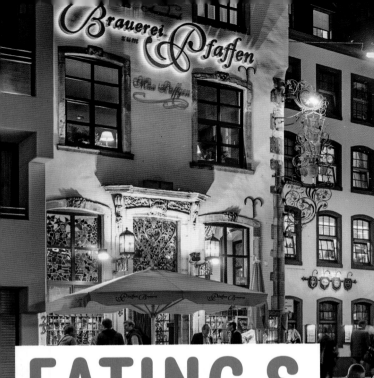

EATING & DRINKING

Do you fancy vegan curry, Peruvian ceviche or a local *Sauerbraten*? This question will pop up every time you choose where to eat out in Cologne, because the city is home to the latest food trends from around the world as well as having its own characterful local cuisine.

The heartiest dishes are served in the Cologne brewhouses – you'll find the so-called *"Halve Hahn"* much easier to digest than the accompanying backchat from the *Köbesse* (traditional serving staff). For example, if you ask for a mineral water rather than a Kölsch, the

All the venues in this chapter can be found on the pull-out map 🗺

Settle in for a long evening at Heumarkt in the Altstadt

likely response will be, "Would you like soap and a towel with that?" Noticeably more civilised are the hundreds of restaurants outside the *Ring*, where you'll find Hawaiian poké bowls, Peruvian ceviche, vegan curries and varieties of tapas from, seemingly, every country bordering the Mediterranean. Thanks to the custom of students and freelance workers, these eateries are usually good value. Last but not least, innovative food concepts have gained attention in recent years, such as food-and-cocktail pairing menus and three-course gourmet breakfasts.

WHERE TO EAT IN COLOGNE

VENLOER STRASSE
Vegan food trends and hip snack bars for party people

MARCO POLO HIGHLIGHTS

★ **JOHANN SCHÄFER**
A modern version of the traditional brewhouse ➤ p. 63

★ **PETERS BRAUHAUS**
Excellent Rhineland cuisine ➤ p. 64

★ **OX & KLEE**
New German Cuisine of the highest order in an unbeatable location ➤ p. 67

★ **NEOBIOTA**
Breakfast prepared by star chefs ➤ p. 68

★ **POKÉ MAKAI**
Hawaiian poké bowls from Michelin-starred chef Mirko Gaul ➤ p. 68

★ **MAIBECK**
Michelin-starred but affordable New German Cuisine ➤ p. 69

★ **ZUR TANT**
Worth a trip: creative cooking with a view of the Rhine ➤ p. 70

★ **LU**
Finely executed Vietnamese dishes at reasonable prices ➤ p. 70

BELGIAN QUARTER
Couple-friendly restaurants and cocktail bars for connoisseurs

SÜLZ

NIPPES

Flora und
Botanischer Garten

Kölner
Zoo

9

51

Lohsepark

Neusser Straße

Innere Kanalstraße

Riehler Straße

Zoobrücke

Konrad-Adenauer-Ufer

Rheinpark

55a

Hansaring

Turiner Straße

ALTSTADT
Hearty brewhouse fare
meets ambitious
gastronomy

ALTSTADT-NORD

51

Köln Haupt-
bahnhof

S

Poké Makai ★

Dom/Hbf U

Burgmauer

Maibeck ★

Peters Brauhaus ★

Rathaus U

Rheinufertunnel

Opladener Straße

Deutz-Mühlheimer Str.

Cäcilienstraße

Heumarkt U

Deutzer Brücke

DEUTZ

SÜDSTADT
Progressive but
welcoming restaurants
with plenty of outside
space

Am Leystapel

Rhine

ALTSTADT-SÜD

Ox & Klee ★

Bayenstraße

Severinsbrücke

Siegburger Straße

Goltenring

55

Sachsenring

Vorgebirgstraße

9

Chlodwigplatz

U

Ubierring

Volks-
garten

Johann Schäfer ★

51

Poller

NEUSTADT-SÜD

Zur Tant ★

Wiesen

400 m
437 yd

BEER GARDENS

1 CLUB ASTORIA

Stroll along the Lindenthal canals through the city's forested park to the Adenauer pond to reach Cologne's most sophisticated beer garden. The beer may be a little more expensive than elsewhere, but you'll enjoy an idyllic spot in the sun and an unrivalled people-watching opportunity. *Tue–Sat noon–11pm, Sun 10.30am–11pm | Guths-Muths-Weg 3 | tel. 0221 9 87 45 10 | club-astoria. eu | U-Bahn: 1 Rheinenergiestadion | €€ | Müngersdorf | ⬚ a6*

INSIDER TIP
Chill out in style

2 BIERGARTEN AM RHEINAUHAFEN

This outdoor branch of the immensely popular Johann Schäfer pub chain offers a view of old father Rhine. *Mon–Fri 4–11pm, Sat/Sun noon–11pm | Agrippawerft 30 | tel. 0221 16 86 09 75 | johann-schaefer.de | € | Südstadt | ⬚ H7–8*

3 RATHENAUPLATZ

Shady trees, reasonable prices and young people from the students' quarter. *April–Oct daily noon–11.30pm | Rathenauplatz 30 | tel. 0221 92 16 06 13 | U-Bahn and buses: Zülpicher Platz | € | Belgisches Viertel | ⬚ E6*

4 STADTGARTEN

Sample beer and cocktails on a huge terrace area shaded by trees. *Sun–Fri noon–midnight, Sat until 2am | Venloer Str. 40 | tel. 0221 9 52 99 42 33 | stadtgarten.de | U-Bahn: 3, 4, 5 Hans-Böckler-Platz | € | Belgisches Viertel | ⬚ E4*

5 VOLKSGARTEN

Atmospheric illuminated beer garden in a charmed location on the edge of a pond in Cologne's most beautiful city park 🐾. The output of the Hellers microbrewery flow from the taps here. *April–Oct daily in good weather from 11.30am | Volksgartenstr. 27 | tel. 0221 38 26 26 | hellers.koeln | € | U-Bahn: 15, 16 Ulrepforte | Südstadt | ⬚ E–F7*

BREWHOUSES & PUBS

6 BRAUEREI ZUR MALZMÜHLE

This traditional brewhouse on the edge of the Old Town serves dangerously delicious Kölsch. Recently, the master brewers have been experimenting with beer fermented in champagne bottles. The adjoining *Höhnerstall* has a large selection of craft beers selected from around the world. *Mon–Thu 4pm–midnight, Fri 3pm–1am, Sat noon–1pm, Sun noon–11pm | Heumarkt 6 | tel. 0221 92 16 06 13 | brauereizurmalzmuehle.de | U-Bahn and buses: Heumarkt | € | Altstadt | ⬚ c3*

INSIDER TIP
Brewhouse world tour

7 FRÜH AM DOM 🚩

One of Cologne's largest *Brauhäuser*, with a huge terrace and seating for 900 people in the different halls. Things are less rustic upstairs in the *Hofbräustuben (tel. 0221 2 61 32 60)*, where large portions of more upscale local dishes are served. Try either a *Deck un Dönn* or a *Stippeföttche schnapps* as a digestif after your meal. *Daily from 11am, Sat/Sun from 10am | Am Hof 12–18 | tel. 0221 2 61 32 15 | frueh-am-dom.de | U-Bahn, S-Bahn and buses: Dom/Hauptbahnhof | € | Altstadt | ▢ b2*

8 SCHRECKENSKAMMER ⚑

The city's smallest and oldest brewery pub – in existence for 560 years! The interior is a homage to the *Rote Funken*, the oldest carnival association in Cologne, which dates from 1823. The waiters still wear the authentic blue waistcoats. *Tue–Sun 4.30–11pm, Fri/Sat 11am–2pm and 4.30pm–midnight | Ursulagartenstr. 11 | tel. 0221 13 25 81 | schreckenskammer.com | U -Bahn, S-Bahn and buses: Dom/ Hauptbahnhof or Hansaring | € | Eigelstein | ▢ F4*

Thirst-quenching Kölsch at Päffgen

9 PÄFFGEN ⚑

Regulars discuss world events over a Kölsch in a lovely beer garden. If you are very hungry, try the *Grillhaxe* (pork knuckle). *Daily from noon | Friesenstr. 64–66 | tel. 0221 13 54 61 | paeffgen-koelsch.de | U-Bahn and buses: Friesenplatz | € | City centre | ▢ E4*

10 JOHANN SCHÄFER ★

The brewhouse of the future: house-brewed beer, healthy variations of local dishes (roasted cauliflower in raisin and black bread sauce) and exceptionally friendly staff instead of boorish *Köbesse*. You're guaranteed a fun evening at what has become one of the city's top destinations. *Mon–Fri noon–10pm, Sat/Sun 10am–10pm | Elsass Str. 6 | tel. 0221 16 86 09 75 | johann-schaefer.de | buses 132, 133, U-Bahn 15, 16, 17 Chlodwigplatz | € | Südstadt | ▢ G7*

11 WEINHAUS VOGEL

One of the last places still to be run for its regulars – most of whom come here to drink beer not wine. Nevertheless, the wines by the glass are tasty and good value. *Tue–Sun from noon | Eigelstein 74 | tel. 0221 1 39 91 34 | weinhaus-vogel.de | U-Bahn and buses: Ebertplatz or Breslauer Platz | € | City centre | ▢ G3*

12 MAX STARK

A brewery with no tourists, music or carnival – but with delicious Päffgen Kölsch beer on tap. The local Cologne cuisine is fresh, high quality, and comes in generous portions. The *Sauerbraten* here is made from horse meat, according to a traditional Rhineland recipe. *Daily from 11am | Unter Kahlenhausen 47 | tel. 0221 2 00 56 33 | max-stark.de | U-Bahn and buses: Ebertplatz | € | City centre | ⑩ G3*

INSIDER TIP
Tradition on the plate

13 LOMMERZHEIM

Chops as thick as telephone directories, smooth Kölsch and a folksy atmosphere – it's no wonder that *Lommerzheim* has earned a reputation as the ultimate authentic Cologne pub. The few outside seats are highly prized in summer. *Wed–Mon 11am–2.30pm and 4.30pm–midnight | Siegesstr. 18 | tel. 0221 81 43 92 | lommerzheim.koeln | U-Bahn and buses: Bhf. Deutz/Messe | € | Deutz | ⑩ H5*

14 PETERS BRAUHAUS ★

A beautiful interior with an art nouveau ceiling and paintings of important local dignitaries on the walls. The house Kölsch tastes particularly good when paired with arguably the best steak tartare in the city. *Daily from 11.30am | Mühlengasse 1 | tel. 0221 2 57 39 50 | peters-brauhaus.de | U-Bahn, S-Bahn and buses: Dom/Hauptbahnhof | € | Altstadt | ⑩ c2*

15 FRÜH EM VEEDEL

A place with a true neighbourhood atmosphere. The menu features classic Rhineland dishes, and you're unlikely to find cheaper beer in any traditional pub in the city; as this guide went to press, it was 1.90 euros per glass! *Mon–Thu from 4pm, Fri/Sat from 11am | Chlodwigplatz 28 | tel. 0221 31 44 70 | fruehemveedel.de | buses: 132, 133, U-Bahn: 15, 16 Chlodwigplatz | € | Südstadt | ⑩ G7*

INSIDER TIP
Budget beer

CAFÉS

16 CAFÉ REICHARD

You will have the best view of the cathedral if you manage to snag a seat on the terrace. But Cologne's landmark will be competing for

Peters Brauhaus

Today's Specials

With your beer

FLÖNZ
Black pudding with chunks of bacon

HALVE HAHN
Rye bread roll with aged Gouda cheese and mustard; literally translates as "half a chicken"

KÖLSCHER KAVIAR
Flönz with onions, served with black bread or a rye bread roll

Starters

KRÜSTCHEN GULASCH
A small bowl of goulash served with a rye bread roll

RIEVKOCHE
Potato fritters served with salmon, herring, black bread and/or apple purée

Main courses

HIMMEL UN ÄÄD
Boiled and puréed apples (heaven) and potatoes (earth), served with fried black pudding

RHEINISCHE MUSCHELN
Mussels cooked with onions, carrots, leeks, bay leaves and white wine

RHEINISCHER SAUERBRATEN
Marinaded roast beef (or horse meat) served with potato dumplings, red cabbage and a raisin sauce

RHEINISCHER HERINGSSTIPP
Pickled herrings with onions, apples, gherkins and mustard seeds, served in a vinegar and cream sauce accompanied by boiled potatoes

Desserts

MUUZEMANDELN
Traditional pastries served during carnival

APFELPFANNENKUCHEN
Apple pancakes are standard fare in the brewhouses

PRUMMETAAT
Plum cake with cinnamon and sugar

Drinks

KÖLSCH
Top-fermented light beer only brewed in Cologne

SPÄTBURGUNDER
Red wine from the slatey soils of the nearby Ahr valley

your attention with the coffeehouse ambience that's reminiscent of Vienna. The pastries and coffee are top class – but come at a price. *Daily 8.30am–8pm | Unter Fettenhennen 11 | tel. 0221 2 57 85 42 | cafe-reichard. de | U-Bahn, S-Bahn and buses: Dom/ Hauptbahnhof | City centre | ⌑ b1*

17 KAFFEESAURUS

An old favourite on Friesenplatz with a stylish clientele. Order a flat white and a granola bowl for a top-notch start to your day. The atmosphere is only slightly spoiled by the choice of music … *Daily 8am–7pm | Friesenplatz 15 | tel. 0221 16 84 17 22 | kaffee saurus.com | U-Bahn and buses: Friesenplatz | Belgisches Viertel | ⌑ E4*

18 HEIMISCH

Fried bread with eggs and bacon, cucumber-and-ginger smoothie and a wide variety of coffees are good enough reasons to make a detour to this place in Deutz. But after settling into the cosy upper-floor space for your breakfast, you may find you want to spend the whole day here. *Daily 9am–6pm | Deutzer Freiheit 72–74 | tel. 0221 16 83 85 63 | heimisch.cafe | U-Bahn and buses: Deutzer Freiheit | Deutz | ⌑ H5*

19 SCHWESTERHERZ

Cosy café in hip Ehrenfeld, run by two sisters. *Tue–Sun 9am–1am | Venloer Str. 239 | tel. 0221 16 95 54 06 | schwesterherz-koeln.de | U-Bahn 3, 4 Piusstrasse | Ehrenfeld | ⌑ D3*

20 485 GRAD

Upscale pizzeria with extravagant pizzas baked at its signature high temperature. Try the "Italian Stallion's Speckbirne", with provolone, bacon and pear. Also, award-winning wines and craft beer. *Sun–Thu 4–10pm, Fri/Sat until 11pm | Kyffhäuserstr. 44 | tel. 0221 39 75 33 30 | 485grad.de | U-Bahn and buses: Barbarossaplatz | Belgisches Viertel | ⌑ E6*

INSIDER TIP Pear on a pizza?

21 FREDDY SCHILLING

High-quality, imaginative burgers sizzle on the grill in a no-frills atmosphere. *Daily noon–10pm | Kyffhäuserstr. 34 | tel. 0221 16 95 55 15 | freddyschilling.de | U-Bahn and buses: Barbarossaplatz | Belgisches Viertel | ⌑ E6*

22 RIEVKOOCHEBUD

In Cologne there's considerable competition to repopularise traditional dishes, but so far *Reibekuchen* (pancakes made with grated potato) have stayed under the radar. In this fast-food joint, they're served with unusual accompaniments such as honey-and-chilli dip or curd with herbs. *Wed–Sun noon–8pm | Salzgasse 6 | U-Bahn and buses: Heumarkt | Altstadt | ⌑ c2*

INSIDER TIP Cologne street food

23 MEI WOK

Vegan Asian food from the wok. The dishes are 100% plant-based, and the

Vegan sushi and more at Mei Wok

curry paste is home-made. *Mon–Fri noon–10pm, Sat/Sun 1–10pm | Venloer Str. 384 | tel. 0221 96 26 97 07 | koeln.meiwok.de | U-Bahn 3, 4 Venloer Strasse/Gürtel | Ehrenfeld | ▥ C3*

RESTAURANTS €€€

🟦 OX & KLEE ★

Daniel Gottschlich is a self-taught Michelin-starred chef. His opulent yet creative menus are a prime example of the quality of the latest German cuisine, and the Kranhäuser on the Rheinauhafen is the perfect location for Ox & Klee. *Wed–Sat 6.30pm– midnight | Im Zollhafen 18 | tel. 0163 8 52 84 55 | oxundklee.de | U-Bahn 16 Ubierring | Südstadt | ▥ G6*

🟦 POTTKIND

Carte blanche is standard procedure in this eaterie, meaning that the kitchen puts together a daily menu depending on the availability of the best seasonal ingredients. Modern German cuisine forms the basis of the menu, with an emphasis on the visual presentation of the dishes. There are plenty of vegetarian options, and both wine pairings and non-alcoholic drinks. *Tue–Sat from 6pm | Darmstädter Str. 9 | tel. 0221 42 31 80 30 | restaurant-pottkind.de | U-Bahn Chlodwigplatz | Südstadt | ▥ G7*

🟦 TAKU

Exceptional cuisine from Asia, with finely balanced flavours and creative combinations served in a zen-like atmosphere. On his last trip to Asia, head chef Mirko Gaul perfected the art of matcha preparation. *Tue–Sat 6.30– 9.30pm | Trankgasse 1–5 | tel. 0221 2 70 39 10 | excelsiorhotelernst.com | U-Bahn and buses: Dom/Hbf. | City centre | ▥ b1*

INSIDER TIP
Japanese tea

27 PHAEDRA

This modern Greek restaurant offers a choice of mezze and classic Mediterranean dishes. These are combined with carefully selected wines – including some labels rarely found outside Greece – and a stylish atmosphere. *Wed/Thu 5.30pm–midnight, Fri 5.30pm–1am, Sat 4pm–1am | Elsass Str. 30 | tel. 0221 16 82 66 25 | phaedra-restaurant.de | U-Bahn and buses: Chlodwigplatz | Südstadt | ⊞ F7*

28 NEOBIOTA ★

**INSIDER TIP
Unbeatable breakfast**

Breakfast is often overlooked. This newcomer has an ambitious plan to change this by ensuring that the first meal of the day is the most important. The evening's New German feel-good menu is hardly more conventional. *Tue–Sat 10am–3pm and 6.30–10pm | Ehrenstrasse 43c | tel. 0221 27 08 89 08 | restaurant-neobiota.de | U-Bahn and buses: Rudolfplatz | Zentrum | ⊞ E5*

29 POKÉ MAKAI ★

Hawaiian poké bowls are the culinary trend of the moment in Cologne. That is partly thanks to Mirko Gaul, who wows fans of creative cooking in his Michelin-starred restaurant Taku (see p. 67). This fast-food joint near the cathedral is his side hustle and offers a variety of changing menu combinations, plus alcohol-free drinks. *Mon–Sat 11.30am–8.30pm | Marzellenstr.*

Poké bowls are healthy, delicious and bang on trend

12a | tel. 0221 2 70 38 88 | poke-makai. de | U-Bahn and buses: Dom/Hbf | City centre | ⑴ b1

30 DAIKAN

Not had your fill of Asian-inspired fusion food and a style-conscious ambience? Then this eaterie is the place for you! The house speciality is an "avocado steak" with a secret marinade. *Daily 11.30am–11pm | Maastrichter Str. 9 | tel. 0221 30 13 59 06 | FB: daikanizakaya | U-Bahn and buses: Rudolfplatz | Belgisches Viertel | ⑴ E5*

31 CAPRICORN (I) ARIES

Lost your heart in Cologne? This cosy, candlelit bistro is perfect for a romantic evening, orchestrated around a menu of French dishes and quaffable wines and accompanied by French chansons. *Tue–Sat 6pm–1am | Alteburger Str. 31 | tel. 0221 3 97 57 10 | capricorniaries.com | U-Bahn: 15, 16, 17 Chlodwigplatz | Südstadt | ⑴ G7*

32 MAIBECK ★

A surprising discovery in the touristy Old Town: sophisticated modern German cuisine (with a Michelin star) that's relatively affordable (four-course menu: around 50 euros). *Tue–Sun noon–3pm and 6–11pm | Am Frankenturm 5 | tel. 0221 96 26 73 00 | maibeck.de | U-Bahn, S-Bahn and buses: Dom/Hbf. | Altstadt | ⑴ c2*

33 GRUBER'S

Fine Austrian cuisine in a relaxed setting. The best *Wiener Schnitzel* in Cologne tastes particularly good when eaten on the covered terrace. Great wines too. *Mon–Fri noon–3pm and 6–11pm, Sat 6–11pm | Clever Str. 32 | tel. 0221 7 20 26 70 | grubers restaurant.de | U-Bahn and buses: Ebertplatz | Agnesviertel | ⑴ F–G3*

34 DER VIERTE KÖNIG

Fusion food encompasses all kinds of combinations, but French cuisine with Indian spices is particularly unusual. Creative dishes, good wines, attentive service and a great people-watching position in Klettenberg make for a memorable experience. *Wed–Sun 5.30pm–midnight | Gottesweg 165 | tel. 0221 48 48 12 88 | dervierte koenig.com | U-Bahn and buses: Sülzburgstrasse | Sülz | ⑴ D8*

35 HENNE WEINBAR

Thanks to all the city's cocktail bars and brewhouses, wine is somewhat overlooked in Cologne. Hendrik "Henne" Olfen set out to change that by opening a culinary wine bar. Accompanying the wine selection are daring dishes, such as aged sardines, and even cockscomb. *Mon–Sat noon–midnight | Pfeilstr. 31–35 | tel. 0221 34 66 26 47 | henne-weinbar.de | U-Bahn and buses: Rudolfplatz | City centre | ⑴ E5*

36 NENI

The restaurant at *25 Hours Hotel The Circle* is extremely on trend, combining Arabic influences with Persian, Russian and German traditions. The roof terrace offers a sensational view of the cathedral, the city and the surrounding area. *Daily noon–3pm and 5–11pm | Im Klapperhof 22–24 | tel.*

0221 16 25 35 61 | nenikoeln.de | U-Bahn and buses: Friesenplatz | City centre | ED E4

37 ZUR TANT ⭐

Not to be confused with the traditional restaurant in the city centre, *Bei d'r Tant!* The creative cooking and great views of the Rhine justify the trip to Porz-Langel. *Fri–Mon noon–1.30pm and 6–8.30pm | Rheinbergstr. 49 | tel. 02203 8 18 83 | zurtant.de | Bus 164, 501 Sandbergstrasse | Porz-Langel | ED b8*

RESTAURANTS €

38 BEI OMA KLEINMANN

Fans love this eatery for the massive *Schnitzel* portions and the local colour. It's just like the good old days at grandma's place. *Tue–Thu 5pm–midnight, Fri/Sat, 5pm–1am, Sun 3–11pm | Zülpicher Str. 9 | tel. 0221 23 23 46 | beiomakleinmann.de | U-Bahn and buses: Barbarossaplatz | Belgisches Viertel | ED E6*

39 LU ⭐

Sophisticated Vietnamese specialities in an unpretentious atmosphere. A cup of ginger-lemongrass tea is always a perfect accompaniment to the modest menu. *Tue–Sat noon–11pm, Sun 1–11pm | Hohenstaufenring 21 | tel. 0221 54 81 34 57 | lokal-lu.de | U-Bahn and buses: Barbarossaplatz | Belgisches Viertel | ED E6*

40 BAGATELLE

Mon dieu, who transported us to a French farmhouse? The dishes are Gallic, the wines are delicious and, if you spend a summer evening here, you'll never want it to end. For all that, you can forgive the sometimes-chaotic service. *Mon–Fri from 5pm, Sat/Sun from 3pm | Teutoburger Str. 17 | tel. 0160 99 44 52 67 | bagatelle.koeln | U-Bahn: 15, 16, 17 Chlodwigplatz | Südstadt | ED G7*

41 ROSTICCERIA MASSIMO

No one can feel lonely at this cosy Italian eatery, where the regular clientele practically sit on each other's laps to feast on the mind-blowing pasta. *Mon–Fri noon–midnight, Sat/Sun 5pm–midnight | Alteburger Str. 41 | tel. 0221 3 48 96 01 | rosticceria-massimo. de | U-Bahn and buses: Chlodwigplatz | Südstadt | ED G7*

42 TOSCANINI

Looking for the best pizza in the city? This eatery is a contender – not least because its pizzas are the size of a wagon wheel! *Sun–Fri noon–3pm and 6–11pm, Sat 6–11pm | Jakobstr. 22 | tel. 0221 3 10 99 90 | toscanini. restaurant | U-Bahn and buses: Chlodwigplatz | Südstadt | ED F7*

43 TANICA

This place is packed every night. The Mediterranean small plates and good wines are totally on trend. *Mon–Fri noon–3pm and 6pm–midnight, Sat 5.30pm–midnight | Engelbertstr. 31a | tel. 0221 2 40 52 71 | rosticceria-massimo.de/tanica | U-Bahn and buses: Rudolfplatz | Belgisches Viertel | ED E5*

44 TAPEO & CO

Small plates and sharing menus are very much in vogue, which means tapas culture is booming in the city. This restaurant has moved from Lindenthal to a much larger location in the Belgian Quarter. Diners can choose from classic Spanish and Portuguese dishes plus the kitchen's own seasonal creations. Try the variation on the Spanish national drink, which adds a shot of Mallorcan herb liqueur. *Mon–Sat from 5pm | Lindenstr. 38 | tel. 0221 82 08 20 00 | tapeoundco.de | U-Bahn and buses: Rudolfplatz | Belgisches Viertel | ⊞ E5*

SIDER TIP
Sangria with a twist

45 TIGERMILCH

Ceviche is the new sushi. If you agree, then you're in the right place. As well as raw fish, this eatery serves the likes of quinoa risotto or pork ribs in Japanese barbecue sauce. A Peruvian pisco sour is the perfect accompaniment. *Tue–Thu 6–11pm, Fri/Sat 6pm–1am, Sun 6–10pm | Brüsseler Str. 12 | tel. 0221 75 98 58 21 | tigermilch.kitchen | U-Bahn and buses: Rudolfplatz | Belgisches Viertel | ⊞ D5*

46 MARIA EETCAFE

Cravings for *bitterballen*, cheese soufflé or "fat chips"? Then this hip Belgian-Dutch restaurant is here to help. The decor is dominated by dozens of plastic Madonnas who oversee the constant flow of Belgian and Dutch beers. *Mon–Fri from 5pm, Sat/Sun from 3pm | Hans-Böckler-Platz 1–3 | tel. 0221 94 65 78 78 | maria-koeln.de | U-Bahn: 3, 4, 5 Hans-Böckler-Platz | Belgisches Viertel | ⊞ D4*

Experience pasta nirvana at Rosticceria Massimo

SHOPPING

Shopping in Cologne is a pleasure, especially in the Belgian Quarter, where the streets are lined with small, independent boutiques. It's a similar story in the Südstadt, where Severinstrasse is a dedicated shopping street.

Within the ring roads, Ehrenstrasse still sets the trend; the brands that have found their way here are only at home in global metropolises. Large department stores and chain stores, meanwhile, can be found on Hohen Strasse and Schildergasse. A unique feature of shopping on the Rhine are the special shops for masks and

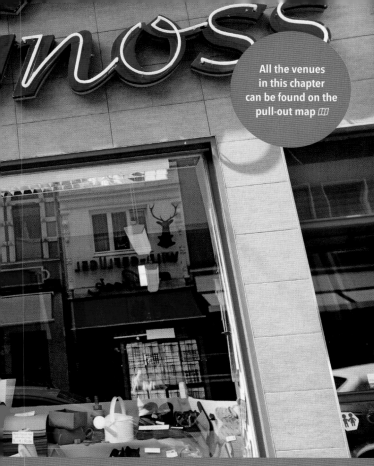

All the venues in this chapter can be found on the pull-out map 📖

Everything's made of felt at Filz Gnoss

costumes, decorations and party accessories, which are kept busy all year round; after all, Cologne isn't only a party city during carnival.

The art scene is also experiencing a renaissance. At the beginning of the millennium, many galleries migrated to Berlin, but some have now returned to capitalise on the wealth of the Rhineland.

In the inner city, the majority of shops are open until 7pm or 8pm on weekdays. Opening times are only mentioned in our listings if they deviate from this norm.

WHERE TO SHOP IN COLOGNE

A57

NEUEHRENFELD

Subbelrather

Köln-Ehrenfeld Ⓢ

Ehrenfeldgürtel

Straße

Ⓤ Venloer Straße/Gürtel

EHRENFELD
Small boutiques with alternative offerings

EHRENFELD

Herrenbude ★ ◉
Ⓤ Körnerstraße
Le Pop Lingerie ★ ◉

Venloer Straße

Innere Kanalstraße

Innerer Grüngürtel

Erftstraße

59

Stadt-garten

Kompakt Schallplatten ★ ◉

Hans-Böckler-Platz/Bf West Ⓤ

Köln West 🚉

BRAUNSFELD

Friedhof Melaten

Carola-Williams Park

Käsehaus Wingenfeld ★ ◉

BELGIAN QUARTER
Trendy concept stores and independent designers

55

Meet & Eat ★

Aachener Straße

Rudolfplatz Ⓤ

9

Ⓤ Moltkestraße

Aachener Weiher

Hohenzollernring

Roonstraße

Hohenstaufenring

Hiroshima-Nagasaki Park

264

Universitätsstraße

55

SÜLZ

ACCESSORIES & BEAUTY

1 DIEFENTHAL 1905

Specialist shop for elegant headgear with an atmosphere that successfully evokes the heyday of the hat. *Tue–Fri 10am–6pm | Friesenwall 102a | diefenthal1905.de | U-Bahn and buses: Friesenplatz | Zentrum | ᗕ E4–5*

2 KITSCH DELUXE

Sophisticated hats, leather handbags, jewellery and other accessories alongside antiques, fashion and gifts. *Mon–Sat 2.30–7.30pm | Körnerstr. 26 | U-Bahn: 3, 4 Körnerstrasse | Ehrenfeld | ᗕ C3*

3 WOHLSIGN

This concept store sets itself the challenge of stocking items that will appeal to people who are difficult to buy gifts for. *Mon–Fri 12.30–7pm, Sat noon–6.30pm | Kettengasse 7 | wohlsign.de | U-Bahn and buses: Rudolfplatz | Belgisches Viertel | ᗕ E5*

WHERE TO START?

If this is your first time in the city, then begin your shopping spree on **Neumarkt** *(ᗕ F5)* where the Schildergasse precinct starts. With 17, 000 visitors per hour, it is rated as Europe's number one shopping street, ranking even higher than London's Oxford Street. To the north is the covered **Neumarkt-Galerie** shopping mall and the **Neumarkt-Passage** arcade – both ideal for shopping on rainy days. On **Mittelstrasse** and **Ehrenstrasse** you'll find everything from designer stores to sports' specialists.

ANTIQUES & ART

4 ANTIQUARIAT SIEGFRIED UNVERZAGT

A rare gem for bibliophiles: an antiquarian bookshop specialising in old art and humanities books – with a total of 120,000 volumes. *Mon by appointment, Tue–Thu 3–7pm, Fri noon–7pm, Sat 11am–3pm | Limburger Str. 10 | unverzagt.com | U-Bahn and buses: Friesenplatz | Belgisches Viertel | ᗕ E4*

5 30 WORKS

Contemporary work based on Pop Art and abstraction – a crowd-pleasing broad portfolio. *Wed–Sat noon–6pm | Pfeilstr. 47 | 30works.de | U-Bahn and buses: Rudolfplatz | City centre | ᗕ E5*

6 GALERIE THOMAS ZANDER

High-quality Pop Art, photography and avant-garde works. The gallery represents the likes of Candida Höfer and Dieter Meier. *Tue–Fri 11am–6pm, Sat 11am–5pm | Schönhauser Str. 8 | galeriezander.com | U-Bahn: 16 Schönhauser Str. | Südstadt | ᗕ H8*

BOUTIQUES & DESIGNER FASHION

7 EHRENFELD APPAREL

Paul Kampfmann prints T-shirts and bags with his own designs, which include Kölsch versions of well-known brands, such as *Superdrüsch*.

INSIDER TIP
Cologne slogans

Thu/Fri 1–7pm, Sat noon–4pm | Venloer Str. 459 | shop.ehrenfeld-apparel.net | U-Bahn: 3, 4 Leyendeckerstrasse | Ehrenfeld | ⌑ B2

8 HERRENBUDE ⭐

This shop doesn't sell anything that its owner, Achim Schmitz, wouldn't wear himself. And it's generally accepted that his fashion sense is flawless. Schmitz pays enormous attention to the fit of each piece and will undertake alterations if required. *Tue–Fri 2–7pm, Sat noon–7pm | Rothehausstr. 4 | herrenbude.de | U-Bahn: 3, 4 Körnerstrasse | Ehrenfeld | ⌑ C3*

9 LE POP LINGERIE ⭐

A self-assured boutique in hip Ehrenfeld specialising in French-style lingerie and accessories. As well as fashion, the boutique focuses on social issues. *Mon–Fri noon–7pm, Sat noon–5pm | Geisselstr. 10 | lepop lingerie.de | U-Bahn and buses: Körnerstr. | Ehrenfeld | ⌑ C4*

10 JOHANNA LUTZ

All the garments by designer Johanna Lutz are exquisitely individual and hand sewn. Customers appreciate her perfect patterns and unusual colour combinations. *Tue–Sat noon–7pm | Gereonswall 13 | kleidungjohannalutz. com | U-Bahn: 12, 15 Hansaring | Eigelstein | ⌑ F3*

11 FAIRFITTERS

Ecologically sound fashion made using sustainable production techniques is sold in two adjoining shops with a garage aesthetic. *Brüsseler Str. 72 and 77 | fairfitters.de | U-Bahn and buses: Friesenplatz | Belgisches Viertel | ⌑ D–E4*

12 TAUSEND FLIEGENDE FISCHE

Colourful boutique offering a large collection of both well-known and new labels. *Mon–Sat noon–6pm | Roonstr. 16 | tausendfliegendefische. de | U-Bahn and buses: Zülpicher Platz | Belgisches Viertel | ⌑ E6*

13 FLORIS VAN BOMMEL

This offspring of a Dutch shoe dynasty treads its own path with some extravagant designs. *Ehrenstr. 39 | de.floris vanbommel.com | U-Bahn and buses: Rudolfplatz | Innenstadt | ⌑ E5*

14 MONSIEUR COURBET

Stylish menswear from top to toe. Find out-of-the-ordinary clothes and reasonable prices. The basement is home to *Groove Attack*, a legendary Cologne record shop. *Maastrichter Str. 49 | mrkoeln.de | U-Bahn and buses: Rudolfplatz | Belgisches Viertel | ⌑ E5*

15 GREENWICH MAN TIME

Lovingly selected men's fashion with an emphasis on fairtrade and sustainability. A life-size image of a young Bob Dylan hangs on the wall and provides inspiration for the shop's aesthetic. *Mon–Fri 1–7pm, Sat 11am– 7pm | Engelbertstr. 12 | greenwich mantime.com | U-Bahn and buses: Zülpicher Str. | Belgisches Viertel | ⌑ E6*

DELICATESSENS

16 HENNES FINEST

A shop specialising in pepper and related accessories for grinding, crushing and serving? Exactly! A few Cologne students started up this niche business. The core product is the Kampot pepper, whose fine aroma delights chefs and gourmets from all over the country. *Tue–Fri noon–7pm, Sat 10am–6pm | Moltkestr. 125 | hennesinest.com | U-Bahn and buses: Moltkestrasse | Belgisches Viertel | ⚏ D5*

17 CARMEN & ROSA

From Iberian ham and Manchego cheese to wine, this appealing shop stocks the very best Spanish products and ingredients. And you can even sample them at lunchtime at one of the pavement tables. *Mon–Sat 10am–9.30pm | Beethovenstr. 22 | carmenrosa-gourmet.de | Belgisches Viertel | ⚏ E5–6*

18 CULINARIA ITALIA

Feel like a picnic in the Cologne green belt? This Italian gourmet deli offers a wide selection of delicious snacks that are worth the price. *Mon–Sat 11am–7pm | Mittelstr. 12–14 | culinariaitalia. de | U-Bahn and buses: Rudolfplatz | City centre | ⚏ a2*

19 KÄSEHAUS WINGENFELD ★

Whether you're after a young, mild variety, a blue cheese or one with whole peppercorns, you'll find it in this pleasingly old-fashioned specialist cheesemonger in the city centre.

To learn more, sign up for the guided cheese-tasting session that takes place on Saturdays. *Mon–Fri 10am–6pm, Sat 9am–4pm | Ehrenstr. 89 | kaesehaus-wingenfeld.de | U-Bahn and buses: Rudolfplatz | City centre | ⚏ E5*

INSIDER TIP
Cheesy seminar

20 KÖLNER WEINKELLER

In the enormous, vaulted cellar dating from the 1920s, you can indulge in a vast selection of excellent wines – it's the only shop of its kind in the country. *Mon–Fri noon–8pm, Sat 10am–4pm | Stolberger Str. 92 | koelner-weinkeller. de | U-Bahn and buses: Maarweg | Braunsfeld | ⚏ A–B4*

21 PRINTEN SCHMITZ

Delicious cakes and pastries, pralines and marzipan creations – since 1842. *Breite Str. 87 | U-Bahn and buses: Appellhofplatz | Innenstadt | ⚏ a2*

22 SCHAMONG

Cologne's oldest coffee roastery still plies its trade from this local shop. As well as fairtrade coffee, the traditional business sells tea and accessories. The barista is regularly voted the best in the region – and he's an earl, no less! *Mon–Fri 9am–6pm, Sat 9am–2pm | Venloer Str. 535 | kaffeeroester.de | U-Bahn and buses: Äussere Kanalstr./ Bickendorf | Ehrenfeld | ⚏ B2*

DESIGN

23 HOW WE LIVE

This light, bright shop sells everything from unique vintage pieces to sustainably produced Nordic furniture. *Mon–Sat 11am–7pm | Beethovenstr. 15 | howwelive.de | U-Bahn and buses: Zülpicher Str. | Belgisches Viertel | ☐ E6*

24 GRÜNBLAUGRAU

Small but perfectly formed shop that stocks pretty prints, high-quality textiles, unusual lamps and other covetable objects. *Wed–Fri 1–7pm, Sat noon–5pm | gruenblaugrau.de | Venloer Str. 457 | U-Bahn: 3, 4 Leyendeckerstr. | Ehrenfeld | ☐ B2*

25 SCHEE

Do you fancy giving your home a makeover without having to redecorate? If that's the case, you've come to the right place. This large shop specialises in posters and prints, but you'll also find cushion covers and wine with unusual labels. *Mon–Sat 11am–8pm | Maastrichter Str. 36 | schee.shop | U-Bahn and buses: Rudolfplatz | City centre | ☐ E5*

26 UTENSIL

Industrial-style design for the home, including original candle holders, classic yellow *"Ostfriesennerz"* fishermen's raincoats and rubbish bins like those you find on train platforms. *Wed–Fri noon–6pm, Sat noon–4pm | Körnerstr. 21 | utensil-shop.de | U-Bahn: 3, 4: Körnerstr. | Ehrenfeld | ☐ C3*

FANCY DRESS & PARTY SUPPLIES

27 BALLONI

Unusual party supplies and quirky table decorations: decorative fabrics,

Printen Schmitz is a temple of sweet treats

There's carnival fun all year round at Deiters

balloons, confetti, glitter, stars and much more. *Mon–Fri 9.30am–7pm, Sat 9.30am–5pm | Ehrenfeldgürtel 88–94 | balloni.de | U-Bahn: 3, 4, 13: Venloer Str./Gürtel | Ehrenfeld | ▥ C3*

28 DEITERS ★

Whether it is for the Rose Monday parade or any other party, here you will find all sorts of fancy dress costumes, accessories and hats on several floors. The main store in Frechen offers an even bigger selection. *Gürzenichstr. 25 | deiters.de | U-Bahn and buses: Heumarkt | Altstadt | ▥ c2–3*

29 FESTARTIKEL SCHMITT

Just seeing all the animal, sailor or pirate costumes will put you in the mood to dress up. There are three floors filled with confetti, glitter, stage make-up, costume jewellery and garlands, where you can shop all year round. *Mon–Fri 10am–7pm, Sat 11am–5pm | Johannisstr. 67 | U-Bahn: 16, 18 Breslauer Platz | City centre | ▥ G4*

MUSIC

30 KOMPAKT SCHALLPLATTEN ★

Minimal techno is probably Cologne's most important contribution to recent cultural history, and the Kompakt record label still distributes music in this genre. The stylish shop has turntables so customers can check out the records before buying. *Wed–Fri 1–7pm, Sat noon–5pm | Werderstr. 15–19 | kompakt.fm | U-Bahn: 12, 15 Christophstrasse | Belgisches Viertel | ▥ E4*

INSIDER TIP
Listen closely

31 GOOD MOOD RECORDS

This specialist shop has vintage records from the 1950s through to the 1980s. The interior space, spread across two floors, is equally retro. Worth the trip out of town. *Tue–Fri noon–6pm, Sat 11am–4pm | Bachemer Str. 170 | goodmoodrecords. de | U-Bahn and buses: Gleueler Str./ Gürtel | Lindenthal | ▥ B6*

32 MUSIC STORE

This musicians' mecca in Kalk is the place where DJs can buy mixing equipment, and instrumentalists can find sheet music and guitar strings. *Istanbulstr. 22–26 | musicstore.de | U-Bahn: 1 Fachhochschule Deutz | Kalk | ▥ K4*

33 UNDERDOG RECORDSTORE ★ ☂

This sizable shop is packed to the ceiling with top-quality vinyl. Main genres include indie, punk, hardcore, rockabilly, new wave, etc. *Mon–Fri 11.30am–7pm, Sat noon–6pm | Ritterstr. 52 | undedogrecordstore.de | U-Bahn: 12, 15 Hansaring | Eigelstein | ▥ F3*

RETAIL ARCADES & SHOPPING MALLS

34 QUINCY

The main draws here are an outlet for the online giant *Zalando* and a branch of the sports shop *Decathlon*. Otherwise, it's worth checking out the photo exhibitions at *Studio Dumont*; the ice-cream stand is also one of the best in Cologne. *Breite Str. 80–90 | quincy.koeln | U-Bahn and buses: Appellhofplatz/Breite Strasse | City centre | ▥ a2*

35 NEUMARKT-GALERIE

When you see the large ice-cream cone by Claes Oldenburg on its roof, you know you are on the right track. Among the 67 shops is the *Richmodisturm*, where two horse sculptures look out of the window. This is based on a Cologne legend: during the 14th century Richmodis von Aducht's husband did not believe that his wife was really dead from the plague, saying that he would only believe it if his horses left the stable and came into his room. A while later, hooves could be heard coming up the stairs … *Richmodstr. 8 | neumarkt-galerie.com | U-Bahn and buses: Neumarkt | City centre | ▥ a2*

36 NEUMARKT-PASSAGE ☂

Besides shops, boutiques and cafés, you will also find the *Käthe Kollwitz Museum* and the *Lew Kopelew Forum* here. *Neumarkt | neumarktpassage. de | U-Bahn and buses: Neumarkt | City centre | ▥ a2*

37 OPERNPASSAGEN

There are gift shops, fashion stores and a piano shop here, plus the largest supermarket in the city centre as well as some cafés and restaurants. *Neue Langgasse/corner of Breite Str. | U-Bahn and buses: Appellhofplatz | City centre | ▥ b2*

SECOND-HAND

38 FLOHMARKTHALLE KÖLN

Bric-a-brac, porcelain, old books, furniture and rarities: You'd be hard-pressed find another flea market with so many treasures packed into such a compact space. *Tue–Sat 1–6pm | Mauritiussteinweg 100 | flohmarkt halle-koeln.de | U-Bahn and buses: Neumarkt | Ehrenfeld | ⊞ a3*

39 PICKNWEIGHT

If you're bored of the identikit fashion available in the boutiques and department stores, then take a look inside this vintage treasure trove, where goods are sold by weight in different price categories. Give yourself plenty of time to rummage and you might track down genuine bargains from designer studios. *Mon–Sat 11am–8pm | Ehrenstr. 60–64 | picknweight.de | u-Bahn and buses: Rudolfplatz | Innenstadt | ⊞ E5*

> **INSIDER TIP**
> **Affordable fashion**

40 SCHWARZER ELEFANT

Do you covet a larger-than-life Buddha statue? Or are you looking for an old oil painting? Whatever you seek, you might just find it here – alongside almost every other imaginable object. The three floors are an extraordinary cabinet of curiosities – a rare treat in the modern inner city. *Mon–Sat 10am–8pm | Hohe Str. 93–99 | tel. 0221 2 57 68 86 | schwarzer-elefant.de | U-Bahn and buses: Heumarkt | Altstadt | ⊞ b2*

41 DIE GARDEROBE

The stock is made up of hippy fashion from the 1960s (with lots of bright colours) through to chic modern styles. Special feature: everything is arranged by colour. *Tue–Fri 1–6pm, Sat noon–4pm | Körnerstr. 29 | U-Bahn: 3, 4 Körnerstrasse | Ehrenfeld | ⊞ C3*

SPORT & OUTDOOR

42 MUSKELKATER

Sports clothing is sold at discounted prices at this specialist retailer. The branch in *Sülz (Berrenrather Str. 340)* specialises in all things cycling-related, including spare parts and clothing. *Mon–Fri 10am–7pm, Sat 10am–6pm | Zeltinger Str. 2–4 | muskelkatersport. de | U-Bahn and buses: Gottesweg | Zollstock | ⊞ E8*

43 GLOBETROTTER ★

This outdoor shop has different departments spread out over four floors with specialist equipment available in *Passage Olivandenhof.* There's a large water sports pool in the basement where you can test boat or diving equipment before you buy. *Mon–Sat 10am–7pm | Richmodstr. 10 | globetrotter.de | U-Bahn and buses: Neumarkt | City centre | ⊞ a2*

> **INSIDER TIP**
> **Waterborne test drive**

SUNDRIES

44 FILZ GNOSS

Everything sold here – from slippers and hats to furniture filling and soundproofing – is made from felt, a

The outdoor specialist Globetrotter takes up four floors in Passage Olivandenhof

traditional insulating material. Felt for hobby and technical use is also available. *Mon–Fri 10am–6pm, Sat 11am–3pm | Apostelnstr. 21 | filz-gnoss.de | U-Bahn and buses: Neumarkt | City centre | ▢ a2*

WEEKLY MARKETS

In Cologne there are 38 regular weekly markets but three of them deserve special mention for their atmosphere:

⁴⁵ APOSTELNKLOSTER

Wonderful flower stands, herbs and oils, fruits and vegetables: a little bit of Provence under the shady trees. *Tue and Fri 7am–1pm | Apostelnkloster | U-Bahn and buses: Neumarkt | City centre | ▢ a2*

⁴⁶ MEET & EAT ★

Every Thursday, market traders, deli suppliers and street-food pioneers set up their stalls on Rudolfplatz. People come from all over the city to browse, graze and sip a wine or two. It's a great addition to the city's food scene, and most of the food is available to take away. *Thu from 4pm | Rudolfplatz | meet-and-eat.koeln | U-Bahn and buses: Rudolfplatz | City centre | ▢ E5*

⁴⁷ NIPPES

The city's only daily produce market takes place in the far north of the city. If you engage in conversation with the stallholders, bear in mind that they speak Kölsch; listen out for *Kätteschloot* for dandelions, *Öllich* for onions and *Sprütcher* for Brussel sprouts. *Mon–Fri 7am–1pm, Sat 7am–2.30pm | Wilhelmplatz | U-Bahn: 12, 18 Florastr. | Nippes | ▢ F1*

NIGHTLIFE

Alongside Berlin and Hamburg, Cologne is one of Germany's top nightlife cities and the undisputed party street here is Zülpicher Strasse.

For a long time, the best bars were to be found in the Belgian Quarter but, due to overcrowding, many locals now go out in this area only during the week. The same cannot be said for Ehrenfeld; its nightclubs are now recognised as world class, and it also has an increasing number of great bars. However, gentrification is a real issue, with many established clubs forced to close their doors in recent years.

All the venues in this chapter can be found on the pull-out map 📖

As the sun goes down, the lights go up on Cologne's nightlife scene

Elsewhere, the Altstadt has traditional brewhouses and tourist-orientated bars. The entertainment focus for Cologne's gay community is the area between Waidmarkt and Heumarkt, and also Schafen Strasse. Meanwhile, the city's neighbourhood pubs still adhere to the motto made famous by local band Bläck Fööss: "Have a drink with us; don't be so stuck up." *(Drink doch ene met, stell dich nit esu an).*

Bars and clubs aside, with around 30 theatres and other performance spaces to choose from, there's no chance of you getting bored in Cologne.

WHERE TO GO OUT IN COLOGNE

NEUEHRENFELD

59 Ⓤ Leyendeckerstraße

Subbelrather Straße

Bumann & Sohn ★ ●

Ⓢ Köln-Ehrenfeld

Ⓤ Liebigstraße

Ⓤ Venloer Straße/Gürtel

Ⓤ Körnerstraße

EHRENFELD
Clubs, bars and pubs make this one of Germany's top nightlife destinations

Venloer Straße   Innere Kanal

Innerer Grüngürtel

Stadt-garten

Zum scheuen Reh ★ ●

Köln West 🚉 **59**

EHREN-FELD   Hans-Böckler Platz/ Ⓤ
Bf West

Carola-Williams Park

55   Aachener   Straße

Aachener Weiher

Ⓤ Moltkestraße

AACHENER STRASSE
Nightlife epicentre with legendary bars and wide pavements

SÜLZ   Dasselstraße/Bf Süd Ⓤ
Köln Süd

MARCO POLO HIGHLIGHTS

★ **MONKEY BAR**
Cool bar with a terrace that offers fantastic views in all directions ➤ p. 88

★ **STEREO WONDERLAND**
Exuberant parties in a beatnik bar ➤ p. 90

★ **ZUM SCHEUEN REH**
Music club with a foresty vibe ➤ p. 91

★ **BUMANN & SOHN**
A hip venue that combines a bar, a club and a beer garden ➤ p. 91

★ **GEBÄUDE 9**
A fantastic venue to catch bands shortly before they hit the big time ➤ p. 92

★ **KING GEORG**
Daily jazz concerts plus weekend club nights in a former brothel ➤ p. 94

★ **KÖLNER PHILHARMONIE**
Acoustics, music, architecture – an impressive combination! ➤ p. 94

★ **PUPPENSPIELE DER STADT KÖLN**
A unique experience for young and old: traditional puppet shows in the local dialect ➤ p. 96

NIPPES

9

Lohsepark

Neusser Straße
Innere Kanalstraße
Riehler Straße
Amsterdamer Straße

King Georg ★ 📍

Gebäude 9 ★ 📍

Theodor-
Heuss Ring

51

August-
Sander-
Park

Hansaring

Erftstraße

9

riner Straße

Konrad-Adenauer-Ufer

ALTSTADT

Brewhouses and pubs
create the illusion for
tourists that it's
carnival all year round

ALTSTADT-
NORD

📍 Monkey Bar ★

Hohenzollernring

Magnusstraße

Komödienstraße

Tunisstraße

Ⓢ

🚉 Köln Hauptbahnhof

Dom/Hbf
Ⓤ

📍 Kölner Philharmonie ★

Rhein

Rheinufertunnel

Rathaus
Ⓤ

Puppenspiele der Stadt Köln ★ 📍

Deutzer Brücke

Ⓤ Rudolfplatz

Neumarkt

LATIN QUARTER

Night becomes day on
Zülpicher Strasse and
in the "Bermuda
Triangle"

Hohenstaufenring

Ⓤ Zülpicher Platz

55

Rothgerberbach

Tel-Aviv-Straße

Am Leystapel

Severinsbrücke
55

Ⓤ Barbarossaplatz

265

📍 Stereo Wonderland ★

9

ALTSTADT-SÜD

51

▲ N
400 m
437 yd

BARS & PUBS

1 BACKES

A favourite haunt of comedians, crime writers and legends of the alternative scene. Cosy pub atmosphere. Live music sessions. *Mon–Fri 5pm–3am, Sat 6pm–3am, Sun 8pm–1am | Darmstädter Str. 6 | backeskoeln.de | U-Bahn and buses: Chlodwigplatz | Südstadt | ⊞ G7*

2 ELEKTRA

This stylish bar is reminiscent of a time when everyone wore white turtleneck sweaters and black horn-rimmed glasses. Today, the clientele is more mixed. *Mon–Sat from 7pm | Gereonswall 12–14 | elektrabar.com | U-Bahn, S-Bahn and buses: Hansaring, Ebertplatz | Eigelstein | ⊞ F3*

3 CRAFTBEER CORNER COELN

The Altstadt has always been dominated by Kölsch, but a young team of craft-beer fans is trying to end this monopoly by offering alternative brews. The bar harks back to the Balkan restaurants that were popular here in the 1980s. *Wed/Thu 6pm–midnight, Fri/Sat 5pm–1am, | Martinstr. 32 | craftbeercorner.de | U-Bahn and buses: Heumarkt | Altstadt | ⊞ c2*

4 THE GRID

This place might just herald a new dawn for the rather neglected party street that, in its heyday, hosted plenty of stylish bars. Sample elaborate and expertly mixed drinks, including stunning mocktails, such as the "Beetray" (9 euros). **INSIDER TIP Fun without the alcohol** *Tue–Sat from 7pm, Sun from 5pm | Friesenstr. 62 | thegrid.bar | U-Bahn and buses: Friesenplatz | Zentrum | ⊞ E4*

5 KLEIN KÖLN

This was once the haunt of boxers and their rather shady fans and hangers-on. A bit of that authentic Kölsch milieu still lingers. *Fri/Sat 9pm–5am | Friesenstr. 53 | klein-koeln.com | U-Bahn and buses: Friesenplatz | Zentrum | ⊞ E4*

6 BARRACUDA BAR

Small club with dancefloor and relaxed clientele. *Fri/Sat 8pm–6am | Bismarckstr. 44 | barracudakoeln.de | U-Bahn and buses: Friesenplatz | Belgisches Viertel | ⊞ E4*

7 MONKEY BAR ★

A contender for hippest bar in the city ever since first opening in summer

---

WHERE TO START?

A reliable starting point is **Aachener Strasse**. From here, you can easily reach the bars in the Belgian Quarter and also the student venues in the "Kwartier Latäng" around Zülpicher Strasse – the party street that never sleeps. At the weekend, hipsters and their hangers-on work their way through the clubs and bars in Ehrenfeld, where the party continues until morning.

Try something different at Craftbeer Corner Coeln

2018. Even the ride in the fancy lift

to the eighth floor of the *25 Hours* hotel is special. The drinks are good and the view over the city is hard to beat. *Sun–Thu 5pm–1am, Fri/Sat until 2am | Im Klapperhof 22–24 (8th floor, Hotel 25 Hours The Circle) | monkey barkoeln.de | U-Bahn and buses: Friesenplatz | Belgisches Viertel | ⊞ E4*

❽ MD BAR

Discreet and stylish, this bar is the epitome of good taste. There's no Kölsch on tap, so the bar only attracts the type of cultured customer that appreciates art installations and excellent drinks. *Tue–Sat from 8.30pm | Marsilstein 21–23 | md-cologne.blogspot.com | U-Bahn and buses: Rudolfplatz | Zentrum | ⊞ E5*

❾ LOW BUDGET

Low lighting, tequila on tap, beer and music – that's it. Yet, this understated place remains very popular, especially at weekends. *Mon–Thu 7pm–1am, Fri/Sat until 4am | Aachener Str. 47 | lowbud.de | U-Bahn: 1 Moltkestrasse | Belgisches Viertel | ⊞ D5*

❿ ROSEBUD

One of Cologne's most elegant cocktail bars. Beautiful interior and expert mixology – reflected in rather steep prices. *Mon–Thu 9pm–2am, Fri/Sat 9pm–3am | Heinsbergstr. 20 | tel. 0221 2 40 14 55 | FB: RosebudCologne | U-Bahn and buses: Zülpicher Platz | Belgisches Viertel | ⊞ E6*

⓫ RUBINROT

With its red-lit interior, this bar preserves its past life as a traditional local pub. Not as chic as some of the city's cocktail bars, but very good drinks and a young clientele. *Wed/Thu 8pm–1am, Fri/Sat 8pm–3am | Sömmeringstr. 9 | rubinrotkoeln.de |*

Weisser Holunder

U-Bahn: 3, 4 Venloer Strasse/Gürtel | Ehrenfeld | ⠿ C3

⓬ SCHEINBAR

Dimly lit bar with psychedelic 1970s wallpaper, funky sounds and a great selection of cocktails. *Mon–Thu 7pm–2am, Fri/Sat 7pm–4am | Brüsseler Str. 10 | FB: Scheinbar |*

U-Bahn and buses: Rudolfplatz | Belgisches Viertel | ⠿ D5

⓭ SALON SCHMITZ

This multi-purpose venue spreads across four houses and a basement on Aachener Strasse. It encompasses the comfortable *Salon Schmitz*, a deli *(Metzgerei Schmitz)* serving delicious snacks, and *Bar Schmitz*, which serves high-end cuisine and hugely popular home-made ice-cream. If you have trouble choosing where to take your custom, you can just hang out at the pavement tables. *Sun–Thu 9am–1am, Fri/Sat open all hours | Aachener Str. 28 | salonschmitz.com | U-Bahn and buses: Rudolfplatz | Belgisches Viertel | ⠿ E5*

⓮ SIXPACK

As a beatnik bar serving only canned beer, *Sixpack* has long been the home of the Cologne avant-garde. Its past glory is still in evidence during the week, but at the weekend it is taken over by sporty types from the suburbs. *Wed–Sat from 8pm | Aachener Str. 33 | U-Bahn and buses: Rudolfplatz | Belgisches Viertel | ⠿ D5*

⓯ STEREO WONDERLAND ★

This place might look like a run-down dive. But when "Wonderwall" starts playing at 4am and everyone sings along, it is, without a doubt, the best pub in the world. *Wed/Thu 6pm–1am, Fri/Sat 8pm–5am | Trierer Str. 65 | stereowonderland.com | U-Bahn and buses: Barbarossaplatz | Belgisches Viertel | ⠿ E6*

16 WEISSER HOLUNDER

The well-preserved 1950s interior makes it worth a detour to this spot in the no-man's land between the Stadtgarten and the Media Park. There's a singalong on Sundays from 6pm with the *Singende Holunder* choir, featuring sea shanties and carnival classics. *Daily from 5pm | Gladbacher Str. 48 | weisser-holunder.koeln | U-Bahn and buses: Christophstrasse/Mediapark | Belgisches Viertel/Zentrum | ∭ E3–4*

INSIDER TIP
All join in

17 ZUM SCHEUEN REH ★

With forest scenes on the walls and a kitschy Bambi figure behind the bar, "The Shy Deer" is one of the most original music clubs in Cologne. There's live football on screen, but also short films, concerts and readings. *Mon–Sat from 5pm, kiosk Mon–Fri 6.30–11pm | Hans-Böckler-Platz 2 | zum-scheuen-reh.de | U-Bahn: 3, 4, 5 Hans-Böckler-Platz | Belgisches Viertel | ∭ D4*

18 SONIC BALLROOM

If you're into punk rock but only want to spend 10 euros indulging your passion, head to the furthest reaches of Ehrenfeld, where the Sonic Ballroom promises a loud, wild party atmosphere. Tattoos and 1950s clothes are standard. *Sun–Thu until 2am, Fri/Sat until 5am | Oscar-Jäger Str. 190 | sonic-ballroom.de | U-Bahn: 3, 4 Leyendeckerstrasse | Ehrenfeld | ∭ B3*

NIGHTCLUBS

19 ARTHEATER

A varied programme of live and DJ events, including performances by up-and-coming bands. There's plenty of drama in the theatre, too! *Times and prices vary | Ehrenfeldgürtel 127 | artheater.de | U-Bahn: 3, 4 Venloer Strasse/Gürtel | Ehrenfeld | ∭ C2–3*

20 BUMANN & SOHN ★

From the cool bar and the beer garden to the overflowing club, this joint has it all. Very cool indeed! A changing roster of street food stalls provide tasty snacks for customers. *Mon–Fri from 5pm, Sat/Sun from 2pm | Bartholomäus-Schink Str. 2 | bumannundsohn.de | U-Bahn: 3, 4 Leyendeckerstrasse | Ehrenfeld | ∭ C3*

INSIDER TIP
You won't go hungry

21 CLUB BAHNHOF EHRENFELD

Hip-hop acts, singer-songwriters and talented musicians about to get their big break: you'll find them all on the programme at this club. Two dancefloors, and street food top it all off. *Times and prices vary | Bartholomäus-Schink Str. 67 | cbe-cologne.de | U-Bahn: 4, 5 Venloer Strasse/Gürtel | Ehrenfeld | ∭ C3*

22 JAKI

This club replaced Studio 672 in the basement of the Stadtgarten (see p. 94). Expect contemporary electronica, jazz and local DJs. *Times and prices vary | Venloer Str. 40 | stadtgarten.de | U-Bahn and buses: Hans-Böckler-Platz | Belgisches Viertel | ∭ E4*

23 BLUE SHELL

As a cornerstone of the so-called and once-proud "Bermuda Triangle", this blue-lit club has been delighting audiences for generations with a varied live programme and reliable club sounds. *Daily 9pm–5am (concerts may start earlier) | Luxemburger Str. 32 | blue-shell. de | U-Bahn and buses: Barbarossaplatz | Belgisches Viertel | ⊞ E6*

24 BOOTSHAUS

According to one British magazine in its annual round-up of Ibiza-style clubs, this is the best nightclub in Germany. It's certainly true that it attracts international DJs, who perform to an enthusiastic party crowd. *Auenweg 173 | bootshaus.tv | U-Bahn: 3, 4 Stegerwaldsiedlung | Deutz | ⊞ J3*

25 GEBÄUDE 9 ★

Hooray, the demolition plans in favour of high-end apartments might be averted! Which means this former factory can continue to live up to its reputation as Cologne's best indie concert venue. Unusual art exhibitions are held in the studio next door. *Times and prices vary | Deutz-Mülheimer Str. 127–129 | gebaeude9. de |U-Bahn: 3, 4 Koelnmesse | Deutz | ⊞ J3*

26 GEWÖLBE

Premier address for club nights featuring all kinds of electronic music in a reliably intimate atmosphere. Folk singers also perform here. *Times and prices vary | Hans-Böckler-Platz 2 | gewoelbe.net | U-Bahn: 3, 4, 5*

Head to Gebäude 9 for live indie music

Hans-Böckler-Platz | Belgisches Viertel | ⊞ D–E 3–4

27 DIE WOHNGEMEINSCHAFT

A venue that defines itself as a "cosmopolitan living room" and welcomes its guests with table-tennis tables and old-fashioned armchairs – it's exceptionally homely and popular. A good drinks menu, carefully chosen music and street food at the door complete the feel-good atmosphere. There's a hostel and a small performance space here too. *Mon–Fri 3pm–2am, Sat/Sun until 3am | Richard-Wagner Str. 39 | die-wohnge meinschaft.net | U-Bahn and buses: Rudolfplatz | Belgisches Viertel | ⊞ D–E5*

28 MTC

Long-established basement club where some big names in German rock music have performed over the years. Metal, rockabilly, punk and hardcore are the staples here, although slightly lighter sounds sometimes feature. There's football on screen upstairs in *Heimspiel*. *Zülpicher Str. 10 | mtc-cologne.de | U-Bahn: Zülpicher Platz | Belgisches Viertel | ⊞ E6*

29 LUXOR

This low-ceilinged, tube-shaped venue has staged some unforgettable concerts over the last 40 years. It is precisely because of the restricted space that the atmosphere at live events is so special. Club nights can be disappointing in comparison. *Times and prices vary | Luxemburger Str. 40 | luxor-koeln.de | U-Bahn and buses: Barbarossaplatz | Belgisches Viertel | ⊞ E6*

30 HELIOS 37

Cool venue in the Helios area of Ehrenfeld (where the fake lighthouse is located). The underground dance sounds are underscored by sophisticated light shows. *Times and prices vary | Heliosstr. 37 | helios37.de | U-Bahn and buses: Venloer Str. | Ehrenfeld | ⊞ C3*

31 DER SCHWARZE HASE

Some people come here to start their long Ehrenfeld night with high-quality drinks; others value the industrial atmosphere and the choice of music. *Daily from 6pm | Heliosstr. 35–39 | derschwarzehase.de | U-Bahn and buses: Venloer Str. | Ehrenfeld | ⊞ C3*

32 ODONIEN

The junkyard-like vibe of this venue located between two large brothels is truly unique: concerts, parties, film screenings and performance events regularly take place in sculptor Odo Rumpf's open-air studio. The bizarre beer garden is filled with Rumpf's furniture, water fountains and fire installations. *Opening times vary | Hornstr. 85 | odonien.de | U-Bahn: 5:Gutenbergstrasse | Ehrenfeld | ⊞ E2*

INSIDER TIP
Scrap heap party vibe

33 TSUNAMI CLUB

If you prefer small cellar venues, then this indie club is perfect for you. Live concerts, lectures or movie evenings alternate, and it is also hosts the *Logorrhoe* spoken-word evening, where all-comers are welcome to perform. *Opening times vary | Im Ferkulum 9 | tsunami-club.de | U-Bahn and buses: Chlodwigplatz | Südstadt | ⊞ G7*

❸❹ CARLSWERK/CLUB VOLTA

Appealing multipurpose gig venue in Mülheim's industrial zone. The music programme runs from soul to metal. At weekends, the hall is used for markets during the day. *Schanzenstr. 6–20 | Building 2.10 (Club Volta) and Building 3.12 (Carlswerk) | carlswerk-victoria.de | U-Bahn and buses: Keupstr. | Mülheim | ⊞ M1*

JAZZ

❸❺ LOFT

Jazz and experimental music in an old factory building. *Opening times vary | Wissmannstr. 30 | loftkoeln.de | U-Bahn: 5 Liebigstrasse | Ehrenfeld | ⊞ D3*

❸❻ KING GEORG ⭐

For the last few years, this evergreen club has become known as a jazz venue, with a full programme of live events. There are DJ sets at the weekend, and occasional spoken-word events. *Mon–Thu 9pm–2am, Fri/Sat 9pm–3.30am | Sudermanstr. 2 | kinggeorg.de | U-Bahn and buses: Ebertplatz | Agnesviertel | ⊞ F–G3*

❸❼ METRONOM

This pub was once a cornerstone of the German student movement known as the 68ers. The yellow, nicotine-stained wallpaper and the photos of jazz greats date back to the end of the 1970s when the former owner, Friedel, took over the prem-ises. His successors still play the original LPs from that time – *INSIDER TIP* **Nostalgia trip** the scratched records are a reminder of the good old days! *Daily from 8pm | Weyerstr. 59 | U-Bahn and buses: Barbarossaplatz | City centre | ⊞ E6*

❸❽ STADTGARTEN

Venue for high-class jazz festivals, pop and rock concerts, lectures and discussion groups. *Opening times vary | Venloer Str. 40 | stadtgarten.de | U-Bahn and buses: Hans-Böckler-Platz | Belgisches Viertel | ⊞ E4*

CLASSICAL CONCERTS

Renovation of the opera house and theatre on Offenbachplatz is due to be competed by the end of 2024 – in theory *(www.oper.koeln).*

❸❾ HOCHSCHULE FÜR MUSIK UND TANZ

Concerts and musical theatre. Almost always free. Also performances in the foyer. *Unter Krahnenbäumen 87 | tel. 0221 28 38 00 | hfmt-koeln.de | U-Bahn: Breslauer Platz | Eigelstein | ⊞ G3*

❹❶ KÖLNER PHILHARMONIE ⭐

The Cologne Philharmonic hosts many international stars, as well as concerts by the Gürzenich Orchestra and the WDR Symphony Orchestra, chamber

The concert hall of the Cologne Philharmonic is a stunning setting for classical music

music and recital evenings. Sometimes there are performances by non-classical artists. *Box office: Bischofsgartenstr. 1 | tel. 0221 28 02 80 | koelner-philharmonie.de | U-Bahn and buses: Dom/Hbf.* You can listen in on orchestral rehearsals for free at lunchtime at the 🐷 *PhilharmonieLunch (tel. 0221 22 12 24 67 | short.travel/koe1).* The schedule is on the website but places are limited, so arrive by noon to secure a seat! | *Zentrum |* ⊞ *c2*

LITERATURE

41 LITERATURHAUS KÖLN

Readings by top international authors in a respectful setting – plus the occasional recital. There's also a comprehensive reference library here. *Grosser Griechenmarkt 39 | tel. 0221 9 95 55 80 | literaturhaus-koeln.de | U-Bahn: 16 Schönhauser Str. | Südstadt |* ⊞ *b3*

MUSICALS

42 MUSICAL DOME

The blue tent next to the Hohenzollern bridge was only meant to be in situ for a short time. However, Cologne residents have grown fond of their musical dome, which has had success with stagings of hits, such as *Moulin Rouge* and *Harry Potter* adaptations. *Goldgasse 1/Breslauer Platz | tel. 0221 7 34 40 | mehr-bb-entertainment.de | U-Bahn, S-Bahn and buses: Dom/Hbf. | Zentrum |* ⊞ *c1*

THEATRE, CABARET & CINEMA

43 ATELIER THEATER

Entertainment by cabaret artists. Upcoming talent and old-timers all like to try out their new material here. *Roonstr. 78 | tel. 0221 24 24 85 | ateliertheater.de | U-Bahn and buses: Zülpicher Platz | Ehrenfeld | E5*

44 COMEDIA COLONIA

Contemporary theatre, cabaret and comedy guest performances as well as theatre, dancing and concerts for all age groups. *Vondelstr. 4–8 | tel. 0221 88 87 72 22 | comedia-koeln.de | U-Bahn: 15, 16 Chlodwigplatz | Südstadt | F7*

45 KABARETT-THEATER KLÜNGELPÜTZ

Political satire, readings, and improvisational theatre on a small stage. *Gertrudenstr. 24 | Box office 0152 04 44 33 68 | kluengelpuetz.de | U-Bahn and buses: Neumarkt | Zentrum | a2*

46 PUPPENSPIELE DER STADT KÖLN ⭐

The *Hänneschen Theatre* presents Germany's only show featuring puppets on sticks – and it's all in Kölsch. If your German is up to it, you're sure to be in for a good laugh – the performances critique current events with the motto, *Wat morjens passeet, kütt ovends op et Tapet* ("what happens in the morning is on stage by the evening"). There are family-friendly shows in the afternoons. *Box*

office: Wed–Sun 3–6pm | Eisenmarkt 2–4 | 21 euros, family shows 13 euros, children 8.50 euros | tel. 0221 2 58 12 01 | haenneschen.de | U-Bahn and buses: Heumarkt | Altstadt | c2

47 RESIDENZ ASTOR FILM LOUNGE

Adjustable leather seats with footrests, a cloakroom and a complimentary beverage on arrival. Whether you're seeing a blockbuster or a classic film, the atmosphere in this luxury cinema is half the fun. *Kaiser-Wilhelm-Ring 30–32 | tel. 0221 91 39 69 13 | koeln. astor-filmlounge.de | Zentrum | E4*

48 SENFTÖPFCHEN

First-class shows and solo recitals. The cabaret stage, which has been around

Much-loved local theatre impresario Willy Millowitsch watches over the Hänneschen Theatre

since 1959, is mostly financed by the drink sales – so the wines are not exactly cheap. *Grosse Neugasse 2–4 | tel. 0221 2 58 10 58 | senftoepfchen-theater.de | U-Bahn and buses: Dom/ Hbf. | Altstadt | ▢ c2*

▨ THEATER IM BAUTURM E.V.

Sophisticated theatre that presents contemporary pieces to a discerning audience. *Aachener Str. 24–26 | tel. 0221 52 42 42 | theater-im-bauturm. de | U-Bahn and buses: Rudolfplatz | Belgisches Viertel | ▢ E5*

▨ VOLKSBÜHNE AM RUDOLFPLATZ ▶

The Millowitsch theatre dynasty reigned supreme at the Volksbühne until 2018. The gorgeous and recently renovated theatre is a multipurpose venue for concerts (usually by local musicians). *Aachener Str. 5 | tel. 0221 25 17 47 | volksbuehne-rudolfplatz. de | U-Bahn and buses: Rudolfplatz | Belgisches Viertel | ▢ E5*

▨ OFF BROADWAY

Expect high-class film programming at this appealing arthouse cinema. And the café is a cultured retreat away from the hubbub of Zülpicher Strasse. Anything that isn't screened here is likely to be on the bill at its sister-cinema, the *Weisshaus. Zülpicher Str. 24 | tel. 0221 4 74 76 79 | off-broadway.de | U-Bahn: Zülpicher Platz | Belgisches Viertel | ▢ E6*

ACTIVE & RELAXED

Soak up the sun beside the Rhine at the Beach Club

SPORT & WELLNESS

BLACK LIGHT MINI-GOLF

Today's gamers don't have to make do with virtual worlds; everywhere in the city, play worlds are flourishing, such as the miniature golf course at 🏌 🤹 *Glowing Rooms (Mon 11am–9pm, Tue noon–9pm, Wed 2–7.30pm, Thu 2–8.30pm, Fri 1–10pm, Sat 10am– 10pm, Sun 10am–8pm | children 12–18 from 10 euros, no under-12s, tickets only online | Venloer Str. 383a | glowing rooms.com | U-Bahn and buses: Ehrenfeld | Ehrenfeld | ▥ C3)* with 3D glasses, black light and 18 holes.

JOGGING

North of the Machabäerstrasse inter-section *(▥ G4)* you can jog along the Rhine promenade for about 4km, past the Bastei and underneath Zoo Bridge, as far as Mülheimer Bridge. Another popular stretch is along the Lindenthaler canals (see p. 55) and into the Stadwald, where there's a traffic-free circuit. If you're feeling compet-itive, you can pace yourself against the students from the Sports Academy, who do their endur-ance training here.

INSIDER TIP
The race is on

STADIUM SPORTS

FC Köln is known as one of the most passionate football clubs in Germany. Whenever a goal is scored at the team's *Rheinenergie-Stadion (Aachener Str. 999 | tickets 17–79 euros | fc.de | U-Bahn: 1 Rheinenergie-Stadion | Müngersdorf | ▥ 0)* the excitement reaches fever pitch.

The second most popular sports team in the city is the *Kölner Haie* (Cologne Sharks) ice-hockey team, who play at the *Lanxess Arena (Willy-Brandt-Platz 3 | tickets 15–165 euros | haie.de | Trains and buses: Messe/ Deutz | Deutz | ▥ J5).* This is one of the best and largest arenas in Europe and

The Rheinauhafen is perfect for jogging

hosts upwards of 18,000 spectators for the most significant matches.

SWIMMING POOLS & SPAS

There's fun to be had at 🎭 🦩 *Aqualand (Mon–Thu 9.30am–11pm, Fri 9.30am–midnight, Sat 9am–midnight, Sun 9am–11pm | adults 2 hrs 19.90 euros, day ticket 26.90 euros; children 7–15 yrs 14.90 euros, day ticket 19.90 euros; children 3–6 yrs 6.90 euros; family discounts available | Merian Str. 1 | tel. 0221 7 02 80 | aqualand.de | U-Bahn: 18 Chorweiler Zentrum | Chorweiler | ▥ 0)* with waterslides, sauna and fitness studio.

🦩 *Claudius-Therme (daily 9am–midnight | 2 hrs 13 euros, weekends and holidays 15 euros, day ticket 29/31 euros, sauna additional 8 euros | Sachsenbergstr. 1 | tel. 0221 98 14 40 | claudius-therme.de | U-Bahn, trains and buses: Deutzer Bhf., then Bus 150 | Deutz | ▥ J3)* is a high-end spa in the Rheinpark, complete with indoor and outdoor pools, physiotherapies, sauna and a beautiful view of the Rhine and the cathedral.

🎭 *Lentpark (open-air pool Mon–Fri 1–8pm, Sat/Sun 10am–8pm, indoor pool Tue 4–10pm, Wed–Fri 6.30am–10pm, Sat/Sun 9am–9pm | 4.90, euros summer price 5.80 euros, ice-skating from 8.50 euros | Lentstr. 30 | tel. 0221 27 91 80 10 | koelnbaeder.de | U-Bahn: 5, 18 Reichenspergerplatz | Nippes | ▥ G2)* has an open-air pool and an indoor pool, plus a raised indoor ice-skating rink.

Sportpark Müngersdorf is the location of the *Stadionbad (mid-May–Sept Mon–Fri 10am–8pm, Sat/Sun 9am–8pm, weather-dependent | admission 5.80 euros | Olympiaweg 20 | tel. 0221 2 79 18 40 | koelnbaeder.de | U-Bahn: 1 Rheinenergiestadion | Müngersdorf | ▥ 0)*, which has eight pools and a ten-metre diving board.

FESTIVALS & EVENTS

JANUARY

⚑ **Loss mer Singe:** potential hit songs for the carnival season are showcased in the weeks before. *lossmersinge.de*

Passagen Interior Design Week: Cologne becomes the stage for high-end design shows. Get inspired by a visit to ➤ *Design Parcours Ehrenfeld*. *voggenreiter.com*

Stunksitzung: an alternative to the civic carnival, with plenty of satirical cabaret and biting political commentary. *stunksitzung.de*

FEBRUARY

Karneval: the largest processions are the ⚑ *Schull- un Veedelszöch* event on carnival Sunday and the Rose Monday parade; the craziest ★ ⚑ *street party* takes place on Chlodwigplatz.

MARCH

Lit.Cologne: international literary festival, with events, including author readings and discussion groups, in the *Literaturhaus* and the *Mediapark*. *litcologne.de*

MAY

c/o pop: a five-day electronic music festival takes place in various clubs across the city. *c-o-pop.de*

Hänneschen-Kirmes: face-painting for kids and carnival bands on the Eisenmarkt. *haenneschen.de*

JUNE

Mülheimer Gottestracht: Corpus Christi procession along the Rhine from Mülheim to the cathedral.

JUNE/JULY

➤ **Edelweisspiratenfestival:** a massive music festival takes place on the penultimate Sunday before the summer holidays in the Friedenspark, featuring reggae, folk and local rock bands. *edelweisspiratenfestival.de*

The "Funkenbiwak" on Neumarkt is one of the highlights of *Karneval*

JULY

🐷 **Sommer Köln:** open-air concerts, theatre, children's programmes. *sommerkoeln.de*

Christopher Street Day: LGBTIQ+ community's colourful demo and street party – part of ColognePride.

Summer Jam: Three-day festival at Fühlinger See for reggae, dancehall and related genres. *summerjam.de*

AUGUST

Gamescom: large video game trade fair, which coincides with the popular *Ringfest* music festival. *gamescom.de*

SEPTEMBER

Jeck im Sunnesching: if you don't fancy partying in the cold during carnival, try this September event instead.

OCTOBER

Intermot: biennial trade fair for motorbikes, scooters and e-bikes. *intermot.de*

Preis des Winterfavoriten: highlight of the horse-racing season at the Weidenpecher Park race track. *koeln-galopp.de*

Internationales Köln Comedy Festival: 120 comedic performances take place all over the city. *koeln-comedy.de*

NOVEMBER

Elfter im Elften: official opening of the carnival season on *Heumarkt*.

⭐ **Art Cologne:** 180 galleries showcase modern art. *Info: 0221 82 10 | artcologne.de*

DECEMBER

Christmas markets: nine Christmas markets take place around the city, from the classic one at the cathedral to a more cosy event in the Stadtgarten.

Silvester: a great view of the New Year's fireworks from the Deutzer Bridge.

SLEEP WELL

AN ALL-ROUND SUCCESS

The Gerling Quarter was long regarded as a problem area, but since the opening of the *25 Hours Hotel – The Circle (207 rooms | Im Klapperhof 22–24 | tel. 0221 16 25 30 | 25hours-hotels. com | €€/€€€ | U-Bahn and buses: Friesenplatz | City centre | ⊞ E4)* that perception has completely changed. The circular building – once the home of an insurance company – welcomes guests with a playful retro-futuristic aesthetic and open-plan design, not to mention a roof terrace with a view of the cathedral. The diamond-shaped, illuminated lift is a popular spot for a selfie.

NEW DESIGN IN OLD WALLS

You'll be sleeping in a former almshouse when you bed down at *Hopper St Josef (65 rooms. | Dreikönigenstr. 1–3 | tel. 0221 99 80 00 | hopper.de | €€ | U-Bahn and buses: Chlodwigplatz |*

Belgisches Viertel | ⊞ E4). The owner-managed house is located in a listed building in the Südstadt dating from 1891; it's quiet and yet central. Breakfast is served in a former chapel, and there is a small wellness area with Finnish sauna in the basement.

ART HISTORY

In the 1980s and 1990s, Cologne was an important player in the European art scene. Innovative artists, such as Martin Kippenberger, would settle their hotel bills with artworks instead of money; some of these pieces still hang in the hotel bedrooms at the *Chelsea Hotel (39 rooms | Jülicher Str. 1 | tel. 0221 20 71 50 | hotel-chelsea. de | U-Bahn and buses: Rudolfplatz | €€ | Belgisches Viertel | ⊞ D5)* The roof area has seven luxury rooms, designed in a deconstructive style.

INSIDER TIP
Bedroom art

Art and architecture at the Chelsea Hotel

GOTHIC GRANDEUR

Modern design and contemporary art meet neo-Gothic architecture to create a unique selling point at ★ *The Qvest (34 rooms | Gereonskloster 12 | tel. 0221 2 78 57 80 | qvest-hotel.com | U-Bahn and buses: Christophstr. | €€–€€€ | Eigelstein/City centre | ⟪ E4)*. Located in the former city archive building (a victim of construction work on the underground system), the hotel has individually appointed rooms and is sure to impress.

URBAN CHIC

The pastel-coloured furniture, bare brick walls and neon signage at the *Urban Loft (180 rooms | Eigelstein 41 | tel. 0221 17 94 40 | urbanlofthotels. com | U-Bahn and buses: Breslauer Platz | Eigelstein/City centre | €€ | ⟪ G3)* are a feast for the eyes. And, with a bit of luck, you'll get a room with a cathedral view, too.

HOSTEL CHOICE

Friendly and good-value, the *Weltempfänger Hostel (14 rooms | Venloer Str. 196 | tel. 0221 99 57 99 57 | koeln-hostel.de | U-Bahn: 3, 4 Piusstr. | € | Ehrenfeld | ⟪ D3)* is located 600m from Köln West train station, on the edge of the Ehrenfeld party district. Breakfast is available in the café for 5.10 euros for hostel guests, or there's a kitchen for self-catering. Hire a lock and key for the lockers or bring your own. Free gigs take place in the evening.

TOO MUCH FUN TO SLEEP

Sleeping car, spaceship, circus – the bedrooms at the *Wohngemeinschaft (17 rooms | Richard-Wagner-Str. 39 | tel. 0221 98 59 30 91 | die-wohnge meinschaft.net | U-Bahn and buses: Rudolfplatz | € | Belgisches Viertel | ⟪ D–E5)* are so unusual that you won't want to sleep at all.

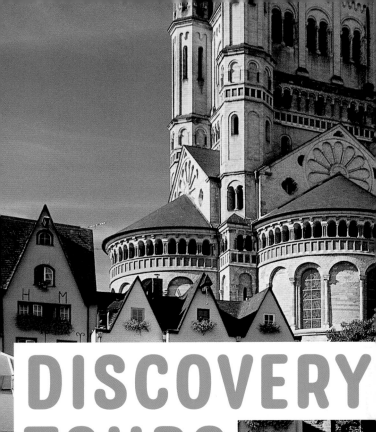

DISCOVERY TOURS

Do you want to get under the skin of the city? Then these discovery tours provide the perfect guide. They include advice on which sights to visit, tips on where to stop for that perfect holiday snap, a choice of the best places to eat and drink and suggestions for fun activities.

Fischmarkt is one of the most picturesque corners of the Altstadt

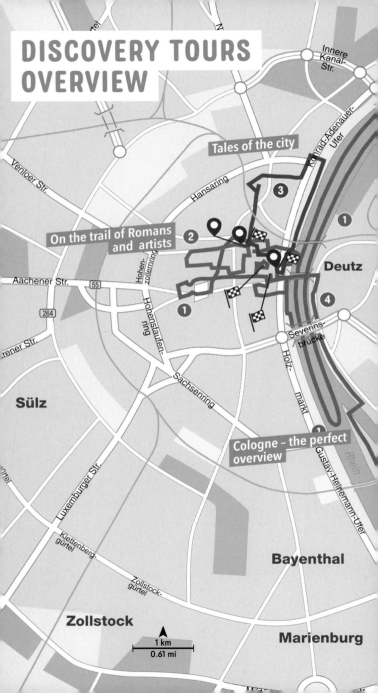

DISCOVERY TOURS OVERVIEW

Innere Kanal-Str.

Tales of the city

Konrad-Adenauer-Ufer

Hansaring

3

1

2

Deutz

On the trail of Romans and artists

Aachener Str.

Hohen-zollernring

Hohenstaufen-ring

55

264

rener Str.

1

4

Severins-brücke

Sachsenring

Holz-markt

Sülz

Cologne – the perfect overview

Gustav-Heinemann-Ufer

Rhein

Luxemburger Str.

Klettenberg-gürtel

Bayenthal

Zollstock-gürtel

Zollstock

1 km
0.61 mi

Marienburg

Cycling through the meadows

❶ COLOGNE – THE PERFECT OVERVIEW

➤ Climb the cathedral for a bird's-eye view of the city
➤ Modern architecture on the riverside
➤ Art, from Rembrandt to Renoir, in the Wallraf-Richartz Museum

📍	Café Reichard	🏁	Senftöpfchen
→	6.5km	🚶	1 day (2 hrs total walking time)

Prices: *KVB-Kurzstrecken-Ticket* (Cologne transport short-hop ticket) 2.10 euros, Panorama boat trip (1 hr) about 15 euros

ℹ️ Expect to pay about 25 euros per person for admission to sights.
⑲ **Senftöpfchen**: admission from 28 euros. Buy your tickets in advance!

❶ Café Reichard

❷ Domturm

❸ Domplatte

❹ Hohenzollern Bridge

LET'S GO UP THE CATHEDRAL!
All routes through the city seem to begin at its most famous landmark, the Dom ➤ p. 31. You'll get a spectacular view of the façade from ❶ Café Reichard ➤ p. 64, where you can fortify yourself with a generous breakfast before you *attempt to climb the* ❷ Domturm *(6 euros)*. The bird's-eye view of Cologne is truly special! There's plenty to see at ground level too: the ❸ Domplatte surrounds the cathedral and is always busy with a demo here, a busker there, not to mention tourists taking selfies in the often-bracing wind.

A RELAXING RIVER CRUISE
From Museum Ludwig on Heinrich-Böll-Platz, steps lead directly to the banks of the Rhine. The Rheingarten ➤ p. 34 sits on top of the tunnel that goes under the river. You now find yourself in the heart of Cologne. *Walk along the river as far as the* ❹ landing stages at the Hohenzollern Bridge. From here, don't miss the opportunity for a river trip on board one of the excursion boats – panoramic views are included in the price!

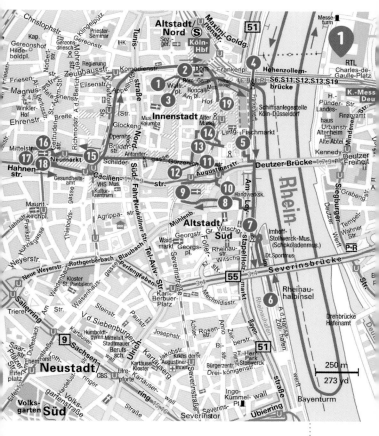

IMPOSING CHURCHES AND GABLED HOUSES

Once you are back on dry land, *walk past the gabled houses of the Altstadt towards the Deutzer Bridge*. The flood levels of years gone by have been marked on the walls of the ❺ Haxenhaus zum Rheingarten (*Frankenwerft 19*). *Continue along the river promenade as far as the* Rheinauhafen ➤ p. 50. *Behind the Malakoffturm turn left over the historic swing bridge onto the Rheinau peninsula, where you'll pass the* Schokoladenmuseum ➤ p. 49 *before you get to the* ❻ Kranhäuser. The design of these three high-rise blocks was inspired by old cranes, such as the ones you

❺ Haxenhaus zum Rheingarten

❻ Kranhäuser

can see a little further along the riverbank walkway. *Return to the swing bridge and cross over Rheinuferstrasse* in order to visit one of Cologne's 12 Romanesque churches, ❼ St Maria Lyskirchen ➤ p. 38. *On the other side of Lyskirchenuferstrasse you'll reach the* oldest building in the city that is still in use: the ❽ Overstolzenhaus ➤ p. 38, whose impressive Flemish gables date from 1230. From there *it's only a short hop over the street known as "An de Malzmühle" to the Lichhof,* the forecourt on the chancel side of the church of ❾ St Maria im Kapitol ➤ p. 38 – look out for its gate of the Three Kings.

INSIDER TIP
Built to last

LUNCH THEN CULTURE

At lunchtime, get a taste of typical Cologne culture at ❿ Brauerei zur Malzmühle ➤ p. 62. *On Augustinerstrasse, take the pedestrian crossing over the tram tracks, in order to reach Heumarkt, with its equestrian monument; then turn left into Gürzenichstrasse.* If you are up for some laughs, browse through the carnival costumes at ⓫ Deiters ➤ p. 80. *A block further on,* ⓬ Gürzenich ➤ p. 37 is the place to see and be seen in Cologne during carnival season: this is where the great and the good of the city gather to celebrate. *On Quatermarkt on the west side of Gürzenich,* you will pass the ruins of Alt St Alban ➤ p. 37, which was destroyed in World War II. The ruins now stand as a monument to the bombing of Cologne. In the ⓭ Wallraf-Richartz Museum & Fondation Corboud ➤ p. 37 you can marvel at masterpieces from art history by the likes of Rembrandt and Renoir. *Diagonally opposite,* don't miss the spacious *Piazetta* (foyer) in the ⓮ Historic Rathaus ➤ p. 35, with its canopy artwork by Hann Trier.

SHOPPING ON NEUMARKT

The Jewish community in Cologne is the oldest north of the Alps. In the Middle Ages, the community lived in the area adjoining the Rathaus; the Jüdisches Museum ➤ p. 36 is currently being built on the site, with completion scheduled for 2026. *Follow Obenmarspforten street to Hohe Strasse. Turn left and head down Schildergasse* to reach the heart of the shopping zone at ⑮ Neumarkt ➤ p. 76. In the Neumarkt-Galerie ➤ p. 81 the motto is: "Shop till you drop."

⑮ Neumarkt

ART TREASURES AND CABARET

Since you are already there, don't miss the chance to check out the artistic treasures housed in ⑯ St Aposteln ➤ p. 44. *Directly opposite the church,* the Amerika-Haus is home to the ⑰ Kölnischer Kunstverein ➤ p. 44, the city's art association, whose rooms are used to stage exhibitions and installations by young international artists. If the weather is good, take a seat on the terrace of ⑱ Riphahn *(Tue–Sat 10am–midnight, Sun 10am–6pm | Apostelnkloster 2 | tel. 0221 99 87 45 77 | riphahn.com | U-Bahn and buses: Neumarkt). From Neumarkt station, it is just two stops on the U-16 or U-18 back to Dom/Hbf.* In the evening, you can treat yourself to a cabaret performance (in German) at the ⑰ Senftöpfchen ➤ p. 96 – as long as you've bought your tickets in advance. The theatre is *only a few minutes' walk from the U-Bahn station with services to the Altstadt.*

⑯ St Aposteln

⑰ Kölnischer Kunstverein

⑱ Riphahn

⑰ Senftöpfchen

Kranhäuser on the Rheinauhafen

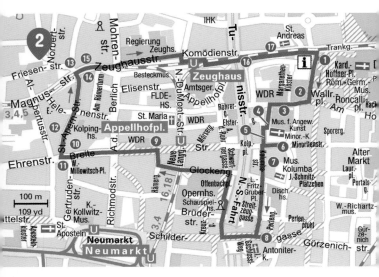

❷ ON THE TRAIL OF ROMANS & ARTISTS

➤ Discover outdoor art
➤ A short trip into the Roman world
➤ Cool galleries with ground-breaking exhibits

📍	Roman north gate	🏁	Roman north gate
🔄	3km	🚶	2½–4 hrs (45 mins total walking time)

ℹ️ Check opening times for the different museums.
Book your treatment in advance at ❽ Babor Beauty Spa.

▼

❶ Roman north gate

❷ WDR-Funkhaus

FROM THE DOM TO THE MINORITENKIRCHE

At the northwest corner of the Domplatte stands the
❶ Roman north gate ➤ p. 31. The *"Nordtor"* was
part of the Roman fortifications and marked the start
of the *Cardo Maximus*, a major Roman thoroughfare
that ran to the south. The architecture of the ❷ WDR-
Funkhaus (WDR broadcasting house) on Wallrafplatz

dates from 1948 and is typical of the reconstruction that took place directly after World War II. *Take a look in the foyer* with its artistically glazed staircase. Café im Funkhaus *(funkhaus-koeln.de)* is another example of post-war design, as is the ❸ Museum für Angewandte Kunst ➤ p. 40, which you'll find *on the street called "An der Rechtschule".* The ❹ Kolpingdenkmal, *a little further on,* is a memorial to the founding father of the Union of Journeymen, Adolf Kolping. He was ordained as a priest in the Minorite church of St Mariä Empfängnis on Kolpingplatz, where he is also buried. The modern and abstract ❺ Stele by Michael Croissant (1993) is positioned *on the corner of Drususgasse and Minoritenstrasse. A few metres to the left, on the pavement in front of the church,* is the equally modern ❻ Plastik by sculptor Carlo Wloch (1992). The statue depicts the astronomer Johann Adam Schall von Bell of Cologne, who lived for a time at the 17th-century court of the Chinese emperor.

❸ Museum für Angewandte Kunst
❹ Kolpingdenkmal
❺ Stele by Michael Croissant
❻ Plastik by sculptor Carlo Wloch

ART AND RELAXATION

Follow Kolumbastrasse to the ❼ Kolumba art musem ➤ p. 40. The building dates from 2007 and its striking design is thanks to the architect Peter Zumthor. After a visit to the museum, it is time for a bit of pampering. *Take Herzogstrasse to Schildergasse to reach* ❽ Babor Beauty Spa *(Schildergasse 39 | 4th floor | above the Douglas shop, separate entrance through metal doors | massages from 59 euros | tel. 0221 27 74 47 79 | baborspa.de),* where you can enjoy a relaxing massage, as long as you've booked in advance.

❼ Kolumba
❽ Babor Beauty Spa

SHOPPING, COFFEE, GALLERIES

Walk back to the Kolumba museum and turn left, crossing over Tunisstrasse to get to Glockengasse. Continue walking past the birthplace of eau de Cologne at Dufthaus 4711 ➤ p. 21 as far as the ❾ Quincy ➤ p. 81, which may tempt you to splurge at the outlet of the online giant Zalando. Ready for a coffee break? ❿ Café Fromme *(Breite Str. 122 | feinetorten.com)* is close by. Head down to the toilets to see the remains of a Roman wall in the basement. From the terrace, you'll

❾ Quincy
❿ Café Fromme

The glockenspiel on the 4711 building plays the French national anthem

be able to see ⑪ **Willy-Millowitsch-Platz**, which has a bronze statue of the popular local actor. *From the café go round the corner to the right on to St Apern Strasse* with its array of art and antique dealers. Young photographers and designers are shown at ⑫ **Art Galerie 7** *(St Apern Str. 7)*; contemporary paintings and sculptures can be found 250m further on, *around the corner to the right* at ⑬ **Galerie Biesenbach** *(Zeughausstr. 26)*.

WHAT THE ROMANS LEFT BEHIND

St Apern Strasse marks the western edge of the Roman town. Evidence of the settlement can be found *on the next corner* in the form of the ⑭ **Roman tower** ➤ p. 42 with its ornamental masonry. *Diagonally opposite* the tower, is ⑮ **Galerie Seippel** *(Zeughausstr. 26)*, where Dr Ralf P Seippel exhibits the work of young artists from Australia and South Africa across three floors. From here it is exactly *1km to the cathedral, along the ancient Roman walls*. A remnant of the walls is visible after one block. For a long time, the *Cologne city museum* was housed in the *Zeughaus*, a former armoury building with stepped gables, but the building currently stands empty and faces an uncertain future.

Directly behind it is the neoclassical Roman foun-
tain➤ p. 41. *Cross over Tunisstrasse once more* and
take a look at the foundations of the Roman
⑯ Lysolphturm on the right-hand corner. Finally, you'll
reach the Romanesque church of ⑰ St Andreas
➤ p. 40, surrounded by sculptures by Ansgar Nierhoff.
From here, the starting point of the tour at the
① Roman north gate *is only a few metres away.*

| ⑯ Lysolphturm |
| ⑰ St Andreas |

| ① Roman north gate |

❸ TALES OF THE CITY

➤ Tracking down the city's legends
➤ A beautiful view of the opposite bank of the Rhine
➤ Eigelstein – where the Middle Ages live on

📍 Statue of Tünnes and Schäl

🏁 Statue of Tünnes and Schäl

🔄 4.5km

🚶 3½ hrs (1 hr total walking time)

ℹ️ Make sure you reserve your tickets in advance for the ❹ Hänneschen Theatre

WATCH PUPPETS PERFORM

The ① Tünnes and Schäl statue ➤ p. 34 *in
Brigittengässchen* pays tribute to these two Kölsch characters, who are the subject of so many local jokes. *A few
metres further on*, the ② Schmitz-Säule is a monument to the origins of the local name Schmitz, which
filled eight pages in the last printed telephone direc-
tory. According to local legend, Roman soldiers used to
meet with young women from the Germanic Ubii tribe
here, and their offspring became the roots of the
Schmitz family tree. *Once you cross over Lintgasse, an
arcade leads to the* ③ Ostermannbrunnen ➤ p. 34, a
fountain decorated with characters from folk songs. *Go
through the passage on the other side of the square to
Salzgasse and then turn left towards the Rhine. After a*

| ① Tünnes and Schäl statue |
| ② Schmitz-Säule |
| ③ Ostermannbrunnen |

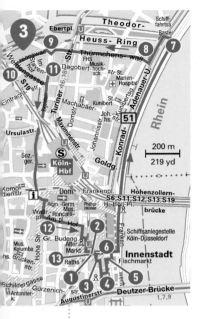

bit, turn right onto narrow Tipsgasse, which will bring you to the Eisenmarkt. This is the location of the ❹ **Hänneschen Theatre** ➤ p. 96, the city's puppet theatre. The puppets perform in Kölsch, but the ☎ children's shows are easier to understand than the other performances and are an experience for everyone.

INSIDER TIP
Watch the puppets

FOLLOW THE RHINE INTO THE MIDDLE AGES

Walk down the steps to Auf dem Rothenberg. As you head left towards Fischmarkt, keep a lookout for ❺ **Rote-Funken-Plätzchen**, a little square with a monument to the city's former *Rote Funken* soldiers, whose troop is now one of the oldest carnival associations. Afterwards, take a break at one of the many beer terraces, such as ❻ **Das kleine Stapelhäuschen** *(Fischmarkt 1–3 | kleines-stapel haeuschen.de | €)*. Now walk north along the Rhine, past the **Rheingarten** ➤ p. 34 and under the Hohenzollernbrücke with a view of the former trade hall (now occupied by broadcaster RTL) and the Rheinpark on the opposite riverbank. The medieval part of Cologne ends at the ❼ **Bastei**, which was part of the fortifications built by the Prussians in the 19th century. But the tower on the other side of the street dates from around 1400 and is known as the ❽ **Weckschnapp** ➤ p. 49. It belonged to the medieval Kunibertstorburg and served as a prison.

LOTS TO SEE AS YOU WANDER BACK TO THE DOM

As you walk along Thürmchenswall and Gereonswall, you will be following the medieval city walls. All that remains of them today is the ❾ **Eigelsteintorburg** ➤ p. 47. Head left along ❿ **Weidengasse** ➤ p. 47, past intriguing bric-a-brac shops and stores selling

❹ Hänneschen Theatre

❺ Rote-Funken-Plätzchen

❻ Das kleine Stapelhäuschen

❼ Bastei

❽ Weckschnapp

❾ Eigelsteintorburg
❿ Weidengasse

Turkish products. In contrast, ⑪ **Weinhaus Vogel** ➤ p. 63 offers a taste of traditional Cologne; *to get there, turn left on to Eigelstein. Follow Eigelstein and Marzellenstrasse south to get back to the* **Dom** ➤ p. 31. On the south side of the Domplatte (known as Roncalliplatz) look for the street called Am Hof and its fountain, the ⑫ **Heinzelmännchen-Brunnen** ➤ p. 33. On Alter Markt, at house No. 24, look out for the ⑬ **Kallendresser** ➤ p. 35, a little figure that sits under the eaves with his naked buttocks on show. *Cross Rathausplatz and then take Lintgasse to return to the starting point of the tour at the* ❶ **Tünnes and Schäl** statue.

⑪ Weinhaus Vogel

⑫ Heinzelmännchen-Brunnen

⑬ Kallendresser

❶ Tünnes and Schäl

A fairytale fountain: the Heinzelmännchen-Brunnen

❹ CYCLING THROUGH THE MEADOWS

➤ Take the tram to the edge of the city
➤ Leisurely circuit through a poplar grove
➤ Riverside route back to the city centre

📍 Zündorf

➡ 17km

🏁 Altstadt
3 hrs (1½–2 hrs total

🚲 riding time)

Prices: 7.40 euros for public transport (KVB tariff 2b for 4.20 euros plus bicycle ticket for 3.20 euros)
Warning: you'll need to carry your bike down a few steps! Bike hire: at the main station *(7 euros/3 hrs | Breslauer Platz | tel. 0221 1 39 71 90 | radstationkoeln. de)*. Otherwise try the KVB bike-sharing scheme *(registration via the app | 10 euros per month, then 1 euro per 15 mins to max 15 euros per day | kvb-rad.de)*.

TAKE THE TRAIN TO THE START

U-Bahn line 7 will take you from Neumarkt in the city centre to the final stop, ❶ Zündorf, *on the southeastern edge of Cologne in just 34 minutes. There is no problem taking your bike on board the train. Once you reach the final stop, hop on your bike and head right on Wahner Strasse. Turn right again on to Schmittgasse and then, two streets further on, turn left on to Hauptstrasse.*

❶ Zündorf

As the road bends, you'll see the 20m-high ❷ Zündorfer Wehrturm *(Wed, Sat 3–6pm, Sun 2–6pm | Hauptstr. 181 | museum-zuendorfer-wehrturm.de)*. It was built in the 12th century and is the oldest secular building in Porz, a suburb that became part of the city of Cologne in 1975. The tower now serves as an exhibition space for professional local artists.

❷ Zündorfer Wehrturm

A VIEW OF THE RIVER

Take the steps to the right of the tower and cycle down Markt street to the south along a tributary of the Rhine. Continue directly along the banks to the end of Oberen Groov, *then turn right onto the peninsula* known as the ❸ Groov, and *cycle through a beautiful poplar grove in the opposite direction, heading back towards the local restaurants.* Hopefully, you'll be able to bag a riverside table in the beer garden of ❹ Groov Terrasse *(Mon–Fri from 5pm, Sat/Sun from noon | Am Markt 4 | tel. 02203 8 55 44 | groov-terrasse.de | €).* You can also explore the inland waterway by ❺ pedalo *(8 euros/30 mins).*

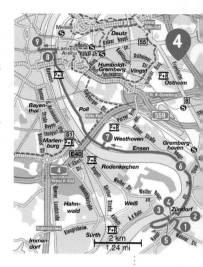

HAVE YOU PACKED A PICNIC BLANKET?

The Leinpfad is a path that *leads past a small marina along the Rhine to the north.* Stop at one of the many small ❻ inlets and river beaches between Porz and Ensen for a rest or a picnic en route.

ENJOY THE SKYLINE

Before you come to the Rodenkirchener motorway bridge, you will cycle through a portion of the ❼ Westhovener meadows, which were once used by Belgian troops for manoeuvres and are now a natural oasis. **Note:** signs warn against leaving the marked paths as old ammunition might have been left behind in the undergrowth. *Continue along the river towards the Südbrücke and the city centre –* either along the raised embankment or down below through the Poller Wiesen ➤ p. 56, an extensive area of meadowland between the river and the sports grounds. Enjoy the pleasant shade as you *cycle under the trees along Alfred-Schütte-Allee until you cross over the old swing bring to get to the* ❽ Deutzer Werft (shipyards). Enjoy the fantastic view of the Dom and the Altstadt. *Cross the Deutzer bridge to return to the* ❾ Altstadt.

GOOD TO KNOW
HOLIDAY BASICS

ARRIVAL

GETTING THERE

Travelling by train to Cologne is recommended. The main station *(Köln Hauptbahnhof – Hbf)* is located right in the centre of the city and is one of the busiest stations in Europe, with daily connections to all major German cities and to European hubs including Paris and Brussels. From the UK, you can travel from London St Pancras to Cologne in less than five hours with one change in Brussels. It's worth noting that some trains (including the service from Paris) stop in Deutz on the opposite side of the Rhine, rather than at the *Hauptbahnhof*, although S-Bahn and regional train services link the two stations every few minutes. For onward travel, there are taxi stands at both exits of the *Hauptbahnhof*, or you can take the U-Bahn (metro); the nearest stops are *Dom/Hauptbahnhof* and *Breslauer Platz*. On foot, you can reach the *Altstadt* or the *Eigelstein Quarter* in just a few minutes.

If you fly to Cologne, you'll arrive at *Konrad-Adenauer-Flughafen Köln-Bonn*, located about 15km from the city centre. Under normal traffic

---

RESPONSIBLE TRAVEL

If you want to mitigate the environmental impact of your trip, you can offset your carbon emissions at *atmosfair.de* or *myclimate.org*, plan the most environmental travel route to your destination *(routerank.com)* and be mindful of your impact on nature and culture once you arrive *(gate-tourismus.de)*. For more information on sustainable tourism, refer to the English versions of *oete.de* and *germanwatch.org*.

The Rheingarten separates the city centre from the river

conditions, a taxi journey from the airport to the cathedral, for example, should take about 20 minutes and cost about 35 euros.

It's just as quick but cheaper and more environmentally friendly to travel from the airport to the city centre by rail: the *S 13* and the *RE 8* services both take 20 minutes, and a single ticket costs 3.10 euros (*KVB* pricing zone 1b). An alternative is to fly to Düsseldorf airport, from where it takes about 45 to 60 minutes to reach Cologne. A taxi will cost approx. 90–100 euros; S-Bahn approx. 15 euros; inter-city train 20 euros.

If you're travelling by car, it takes about eight hours to drive from London to Cologne via the Channel Tunnel. In the city, you'll quickly notice that Cologne still prioritises car use over everything else, which means that during rush hour, the ring roads and all the arterial roads are hopelessly clogged with traffic. If you still plan to travel by car, bear in mind that only cars with green eco-stickers are permitted to drive in the city centre and parking in the city's multistorey car parks costs upwards of 16 euros per day; the car park on Heumarkt is good value and central.

Eurolines and *Flixbus* operate coach services between the UK and Cologne, via Köln-Bonn airport.

IMMIGRATION

EU citizens are not subject to any entry requirements, meaning they can enter, stay and work in Germany without needing a visa. UK citizens with a valid passport can travel to any country in the Schengen area (including Germany) for up to 90 days within a 180-day period without a visa. For further details, see the UK Government's travel advice for Germany at *gov.uk*. US nationals can visit Germany for up to 90 days without a visa for tourism, business and short-term study, although the rules are due to change in 2025 *(see etiaseu.com/us-citizens)*. Nationals of other countries should refer to official travel advice from their own government.

GETTING AROUND

BIKE HIRE

The flood of bike rental schemes shows no sign of abating in Cologne; this positive development is supported by the ever-growing network of bicycle lanes. As well as regional suppliers, the city's public transport organisation, *KVB*, runs a *Bike-Sharing-Service (register through the app, 10 euros per month registration, plus 1 euro per 15 mins | kvb-rad.de)*. German Railways offers a similar *Call a Bike (callabike.de)* service. Register on the app and then pay 1 euro per 15 minutes up to a maximum of 9 euros per day.

Radstation Köln (Markmannsgasse/ Rheingarten, at the Deutzer bridge and at Hauptbahnhof/Breslauer Platz | tel. 0221 1 39 71 90 | radstationkoeln. de | U-Bahn and buses: Heumarkt | Altstadt | ▥ G5) charges 7 euros for three hours' bike hire or 14 euros for a whole day. A three-hour guided cycle tour (in German) starts from here at 1.30pm daily *(April–Oct, 26 euros incl. bike hire)*. Guided cycle tours in English are available by appointment.

E-SCOOTER

For the last few years, e-scooters have been a feature of the cityscape. Around 2,000 of them were introduced to the city by three separate companies: *Lime (li.me/de)*, *Tier (tier.app)* and *Bolt (bolt.eu)*. All three work in similar ways: customers must download an app in order to receive a registration code. Once they have registered their payment details (credit card number or Paypal), then they can use the app to locate the e-scooters and use them for short trips in designated areas. Customers are charged 1 euro per journey plus 15 cents per minute.

PARKING

The car park at the cathedral costs 2.40 euros per hour, up to a maximum of 24 euros per day *(evening rate from 7pm, 1 euro/hr.)*. Other places in the inner city charge 1.80–3 euros per hour (for details, see *short.travel/ koe3*). Watch out for the temporary parking restrictions that are enforced on the eve of the carnival and street festivals: the tow-away truck appears faster than you think! Blocking a bicycle path or a fire engine parking space is also a towable offence.

PUBLIC TRANSPORT

In view of the traffic jams on the motorway ring road and the parking problems in the inner city, using public transport in the Cologne-Bonn-Düsseldorf region is highly recommended. A *Kurzticket* is valid for short journeys of up to three stops and costs 2.10 euros; a standard ticket is 3.20 euros; a four-journey ticket,

Underground art at Äussere Kanalstrasse station

12.80 euros, and a 24-hour ticket, 7.70 euros. These prices apply across the whole network, so it doesn't matter whether you use the DB (German Railways) regional express, the S-Bahn (commuter rail service), Cologne's U-Bahn (metro) and buses or regional transport services. Note that there is no rail service between Heumarkt and Severinstrasse until at least 2025 due to a serious incident that led to the collapse of the city archive, among other things.

Tickets can be bought at the ticket counters in the main train station; in the KVB passenger centres (e.g. at Neumarkt); and at ticket machines in U-Bahn stations or on board trains. ☛ A practical alternative is to use the transport companies' apps, which require registration but save you up to 10 per cent on the standard ticket prices. The app's *Normalticket* allows

you travel on the network for 90 minutes with as many changes as you like. You can also buy tickets to Düsseldorf, Aachen or Bonn. For information, refer to *kvb.koeln*.

Buses to the suburbs and surrounding areas depart from *Hauptbahnhof/ Breslauer Platz (tel. 0221 1 63 70 | rvk. de | Altstadt | ⊞ G4)*.

TAXI

Taxi fares start at 4.90 euros, then charge 2.60 euros per kilometre up to 7km and 1.80 euros for every kilometre after that; waiting time is charged at 0.50 euros per minute. Alternative services offering lower fares, such as Uber, do exist in Cologne but aren't as ubiquitous as in other cities. Note that taxis are hard to come by on Christmas Eve, New Year's Eve and during carnival; try calling *Taxi-Ruf Köln (tel. 0221 28 82)*.

EMERGENCIES ESSENTIALS

EMERGENCY SERVICES

Emergency dentist: *tel. 01805 98 67 00* | *zahnarzt-notdienst.de*
Emergency doctor: *tel. 11 61 17* | *116117.de*
Emergency pharmacy: *aponet.de*
Fire brigade: *tel 112*
Police: *tel. 110*

CONSULATES
BRITISH CONSULATE GENERAL

Willi-Becker-Allee 10 | *40227 Düsseldorf* | *tel. 0211 9 44 80* | *gov.uk/ contact-consulate-dusseldorf*

CANADIAN CONSULATE

Benrather Str. 8 | *40213 Düsseldorf* | *tel. 0211 17 21 70* | *germany.gc.ca*

US CONSULATE GENERAL

Willi-Becker-Allee 10 | *40227 Düsseldorf* | *tel. 0211 7 88 89 27* | *de.usembassy.gov/de*

HEALTH INSURANCE

UK citizens should apply for a free UK Global Health Insurance Card (GHIC) before leaving the UK, which entitles you to state-provided medical treatment. This is not a substitute for private travel insurance, as it does not cover all medical eventualities and is only valid for state healthcare, not private treatment. Travellers from all countries should take out comprehensive travel insurance before departure that is suitable for their needs.

ACCOMMODATION

Prices for overnight stays are about average for a German city. The nicest places are the independently managed hotels, such as *The Qvest* or *Hopper St Josef*, and the smaller chain hotels, such as *25 Hours Hotel – The Circle* (for all, see p. 104–105).

When you're planning your stay, bear in mind that Cologne's hotel rooms are fully booked during its frequent trade fairs and prices go through the roof. The same applies to carnival week when accommodation is often booked up months in advance.

CARNIVAL

Normal service shuts down in Cologne during carnival week; all the city's authorities and official bodies are closed or only have skeleton staff. If you want to join in with the festivities at the street parties or in the pubs, then it is best to leave your credit card and valuable jewellery in the hotel safe and only take cash in small notes. **Real carnival pros reactivate an old mobile handset for the carnival,** or they just leave their mobile phone at home. If you do carry a mobile phone or wallet, be sure to keep it hidden and close to your body rather than in a coat pocket; thieves will take advantage of anyone who doesn't take extra care of their possessions.

INSIDER TIP
Use an old phone

Be sure to dress warmly for the four-hour Rosenmontag parade. The procession route is 6km long and attracts up to 1.5 million spectators, so you'll need to get to your chosen spot early in order to get a good view of the action. You'll also need to show patience if you want to get into one of the carnival pubs; waits of several hours are not unusual.

Tickets for organised events, such as shows and balls, are usually only available online in advance *(koelnerkarneval. de)*, which makes it easier for out-of-towners to participate, although some carnival clubs and organisations manage their own ticket sales.

CITY CARD

The *KölnCard* offers free travel on public transport, reduced admission to many Cologne museums plus cheaper tickets for boat trips on the Rhine and for some theatres. In addition, there's a 50 per cent reduction on guided tours and discounts in many shops and restaurants. When these are added up, you quickly recoup the price of the card: 9 euros per person for 24 hours or 18 euros for 48 hours. Groups of up to five people pay only a little more than double the single person price (19/38 euros). You can find a list of all the discounts and other information at *koelntourismus.de*.

CUSTOMS

EU citizens may import and export goods for their own personal use tax-free. Duty-free limits for non-EU citizens are 2 litres of wine, 1 litre of spirits and 200 cigarettes.

FINES

In order to keep the city clean and tidy, the city authorities impose stiff penalties for a number of offences. You can be fined up to 250 euros for allowing your dog into a playground or onto a sports field, and at least 100 euros if it fouls the pavement. Dropping your used chewing gum on the street is not allowed and may result in a 35-euro fine. Throwaway barbecues are not permitted in public green spaces – the fine for using one is 300 euros.

RIVER TRIPS

The best-known boat trip is the *Müllemer Bőőtche* run by the *Dampfschifffahrt Colonia (mid-March–Oct 10am–5.30pm every 45 mins Sat/Sun, less frequently Mon–Fri | 15 euros | tel. 0221 2 57 42 25 | dampf schiffahrt-colonia.de | Mülheim | ▢ 0)*. A one-hour round trip takes you from the Hohenzollern bridge to the zoo to Iheim and back.

The *Köln-Düsseldorfer Deutsche Rheinschifffahrt AG* offers a one-hour trip from Frankenwerft/Rheingarten (between the Hohenzollern and Deutzer bridges) aboard two ships, the *MS Jan von Werth* and the *MS Drachenfels (Panorama trip 15 euros; evening trip Mon–Thu 8–10pm, 22 euros; day trip to Zons 46 euros | for timetable info, see k-d.com | tel. 0221 2 08 83 18 | Altstadt | ▢ G5)*.

The *KölnTourist Personenschiffahrt (March–Oct departures 11.15am–5.15pm, Nov/Dec from noon | 15 euros | koelntourist.net | Altstadt | ▢ G4)* leaves from Konrad-Adenauer-Ufer for a one-hour trip to Rodenkirchen.

HOW MUCH DOES IT COST?

Kölsch	*2 euros*
	for a 0.2-litre glass
Bike hire	*9 euros*
	per day
U-Bahn	*7.70 euros*
	for a day ticket
Carnival	*48 euros*
	for a seat in the
	"Lachende
	Kölnarena"
Coffee	*2.80/4.50 euros*
	for a filter coffee or a
	latte
"Halve Hahn"	*4.50 euros*
	in a traditional
	brewhouse

SIGHTSEEING TOURS

A large variety of guided tours of the city are available. *Cologne Tourism (cologne-tourism.com/booking/guided-tours)* has plenty of options to choose from on its website, including several in English, such as the perennially popular "Highlights of Cologne" walking tour. Other private companies also provide tours in English, although these are often only available as group bookings. Among the best is *Guided Tours Cologne (ff-guided-tours. cologne)*. Group tours of Cologne's breweries are also available.

CCS Busreisen GmbH runs open-top bus tours – either as continuous tours or hop-on hop-off options *(daily 10am, noon, 2pm, April–Oct also Fri/ Sat 4pm | from 14.40 euros | from Köln Tourismus Service-Center | Kardinal-Höffner-Platz 1 | tel. 0221 9 79 25 70 | ccs-busreisen.de | U-Bahn, S-Bahn and buses: Dom/Hbf.).*

Streetart, Graffiti and other urban art forms are the focus of the work done by *Cityleaks (7.50–12 euros | for details, see cityleaks-festival.de)*. From April to September, the team runs regular tours (on foot or by bike) through the Belgian Quarter, Ehrenfeld and Nippes.

Domforum (Roncalliplatz 2 | tel. 0221 92 58 47 20 | domforum.de | U-Bahn, S-Bahn and buses: Dom/Hbf. | City centre | ☐☐ G4) runs guided tours of the cathedral and the city's 12 Romanesque churches. Check the website or visit *Domforum* in person for details.

With *Stattreisen (12 euros | tel. 0221 7 32 51 13 | for details, see stattreisen-koeln.de)* you can discover another side of Cologne, away from the tourist clichés. Their themed tours include "Cologne in Tales and Legends" and "The Jews of Cologne".

TICKETS

Tickets for concerts, theatre performances, sporting events and musicals can be bought from the *Theaterkasse Neumarkt (Mon–Sat 10am–6.30pm | in the subterranean shopping arcade | tel. 0221 42 07 60 00 | theaterkasse-neumarkt.de | U-Bahn and buses: Neumarkt | City centre | ☐☐ F5).*

Tickets are also available online in advance through *koelnticket.de (tel. 0221 28 01)*. For *Kölner Philharmonie* tickets, refer to the website or call the ticket hotline *(koelner-philharmonie. de | tel. 0221 28 02 80)*.

TIPPING

If you are satisfied with the service in a restaurant or bar you should tip between 10 and 15 per cent. Some taxi drivers will round-up the fare, but this is not standard practice. *Köbesse* (brewhouse serving staff) are officially only allowed to accept alcohol-free drinks from customers. City officials, including those working in museums or as tour guides, are not permitted to accept tips.

TOURIST INFORMATION

Directly opposite the cathedral is the *Cologne Tourism Service-Center (Mon–Sat 9am–7pm, Sun and public hols 10am–5pm | tel. 0221 34 64 30 | info@koelntourismus.de | koeln tourismus.de | Altstadt | ⌑ F4)*, which also has a souvenir shop. This is the city's official tourist information office

and it offers all kinds of guided tours on various local themes; the brewery tours are particularly popular (see p. 128).

A calendar of the most important events is published online at *stadt revue.de*; the official site for the city authorities is *stadt-koeln.de*; for tickets to shows, etc., see *koelnticket. de;* and for museums and galleries, visit *koelngalerien.de* and *museen koeln.de*; for trade fairs, *koelnmesse. de*; for carnival, *koelnerkarneval.de*.

WEATHER

The winters in Cologne are milder and less snowy than in some parts of Germany, while the summers in this low-lying area can be oppressively hot and humid. Overall, however, this is a year-round destination.

WEATHER IN COLOGNE

	JAN	FEB	MARCH	APRIL	MAY	JUNE	JULY	AUG	SEPT	OCT	NOV	DEC
Daytime temperature	4°	6°	10°	14°	19°	22°	24°	24°	20°	14°	9°	5°
Night-time temperature	-1°	0°	2°	5°	8°	12°	14°	14°	11°	7°	4°	0°
Sunshine hours/day	2	2	4	5	6	7	6	5	5	4	2	2
Rainy days/month	18	15	13	17	13	13	14	14	14	16	18	17

HOLIDAY VIBES
FOR RELAXATION & CHILLING

FOR BOOKWORMS & FILM BUFFS

📖 DEATH AND THE DEVIL

A novel by Frank Schätzing who achieved international fame with his thriller *The Swarm*. *Death and the Devil* is set in 13th-century Cologne and is a fascinating portrayal of medieval life and the political events of the time with a plot against the Archbishop of Cologne. English version available in paperback and on Kindle.

🎥 EDELWEISS PIRATES

Niko von Glasow's 2005 emotional film centres around a youth resistance group during World War II. The action takes place in and around Cologne.

📖 COLOGNE CRIME

There are dozens of crime novels set in Cologne and surrounding areas but not many are available in English. The "Judith Krieger" stories by local author Gisa Klönne are an exception.

🎥 CHARLIE MARIANO – LAST VISITS

A film by Axel Engstfeld (2013) about a Boston-based jazz saxophonist, who spent the final 20 years of his life in Cologne.

PLAYLIST ON SHUFFLE

0:58

II BAP – SÜDSTADT, VERZÄLL NIX
Wolfgang Niedecken and band, probably Cologne's most successful musical export, take on the topic of gentrification in the city

▶ **QUERBEAT** –
NIE MEHR FASTELOVEND
Upbeat example of the new generation of bands that write and perform in the local dialect

▶ **BLÄCK FÖÖSS** –
BEI UNS IM VEEDEL
The ultimate expression of Kölsch identity

▶ **CAT BALLOU** – ET JITT KEI WOOD
This ballad tugs on the heartstrings of even the most unsentimental Cologne citizen

▶ **HÖHNER** –
MER STONN ZU DIR, FC KÖLLE
Supporting FC Cologne through the good times and the bad

Your holiday soundtrack can be found on Spotify under MARCO POLO Cologne

Or scan this code with the Spotify app

ONLINE

VISIT KÖLN
The tourist board's official website has practical information, articles, an events calendar and links to a booking site for city hotels. You can also buy the KölnCard for discounts on many sights and attractions.
www.cologne-tourism.com

GERMANY TRAVEL BLOG
Stephan Drescher guides you around Cologne, Düsseldorf and Hamburg with useful information, photos and tips.
germanytravel.blog/cities/cologne/

RAUSGEGANGEN
German and English website with events information and articles on where to go and what to do in the city.
rausgegangen.de

KVB
The transport authority's app and website have timetables and trip-planning tools as well as a ticket shop for buses and trains in and around Cologne. There's also information about bike hire, car-sharing and taxi services in the city.
www.kvb.koeln/en

TRAVEL
PURSUIT
THE MARCO POLO HOLIDAY QUIZ

Do you know what makes Cologne tick? Test your knowledge of the idiosyncrasies and eccentricities of the city and its people. The answers are at the foot of the page, with further information on pages 20–25.

❶ Where is Kölsch brewed?
a) Exclusively in Cologne and the Rhineland
b) Throughout Germany
c) In many places around the world but, in Germany, it's only brewed in and around Cologne

❷ What do Cologne citizens look forward to on 11 November?
a) This is the date on which FC Köln usually reach their top form
b) You can buy carnival costumes tax free from this date until Christmas
c) It marks the beginning of carnival season

❸ What is the meaning of *Klüngel*?
a) Illegal deals that still go on behind the scenes
b) Unfair laws that give the advantage to outsiders
c) Sewers that date back to Roman times

❹ Eau de Cologne was originally created as a remedy for which ailment?
a) Body odour
b) Headaches
c) Knobbly knees

REWE supermarket in Cologne's city centre

❺ Which local saying sums up Cologne's tolerant attitude?
a) *Jeder Jeck es anders* – "every fool is different"
b) *Dat Schönste wat mer han … is unser Veedel* – "the most important thing in life is your neighbourhood"
c) *Drink doch ene met, stell dich nit esu an* – "Go on, have a drink with us; don't be so stuck up"

❻ Which form of transport still gets priority in the city?
a) The U-Bahn
b) The bicycle
c) The car

❼ Who are Cologne's largest employers today?
a) Creative industries
b) REWE Group industry
c) Ford Motor Company

INDEX

WE WANT TO HEAR FROM YOU!

Did you have a great holiday? Is there something on your mind? Whatever it is, let us know! Whether you want to praise the guide, alert us to errors or give us a personal tip – MARCO POLO would be pleased to hear from you.
Please contact us by email:

sales@heartwoodpublishing.co.uk

We do everything we can to provide the very latest information for your trip. Nevertheless, despite all of our authors' thorough research, errors can creep in. MARCO POLO does not accept any liability for this.

PICTURE CREDITS
Cover photo: Cologne Cathedral (Schapowalow: F. Carovillano)
Photos: R. Hackenberg (10, 11, 90, 106/107); huber-images: Bäck (21), G. Croppi (36/37), Gräfenhain (35, 113, 119), G. Gräfenhain (2/3), H. Klaes (57), L. Kornblum (12/13, 102/103), S Lubenow (6/7), S. Lubenow (4, 50, 58/59), H. - P. Merten (26/27), M. Rellini (front outside flap, front inside flap, 1, 25), R. Schmid (45), C. Seba (39, 122/123); R. Johnen (135); L. Kornblum (63, 83); Laif: R. Brunner (47), W. Gollhardt (104/105), Huber (42/43), Jung (54), Linke (31, laif: Linke (95); Laif: M. Linke (22, 79), R. Müllenmeister (126), T. Rabasch (80), Reinicke (125), K. Schoene (52), D. Schwelle (130/131), Zanettini (98/99); K. Lindemann (17, 89); mauritius images: W. Dieterich (116); mauritius images : W. Otto (96/97); mauritius images/Alamy: K. Sriskandan (8); mauritius images/Alamy/Alamy Stock Photos: S. Ettmer (14/15), E. Teister (9); mauritius images/Cavan Images (68); mauritius images/Travel Collection (72/73); mauritius images/Westende61: C. Hernandez (100/101), A. Tamboly (84/85); A. Siggelkow (64, 71, 92); S. Troll (67); Rick Neves/Shutterstock.com (132/133)

4th Edition – fully revised and updated 2024
Worldwide Distribution: Heartwood Publishing Ltd, Bath, United Kingdom
www.heartwoodpublishing.co.uk

Authors: Ralf Johnen, Jürgen Raap
Editor: Jens Bey
Picture editor: Gabriele Forst
Cartography: © MAIRDUMONT, Ostfildern (108–109, 111, 114, 118, 121, outer wallet, pull-out map);
© MAIRDUMONT, Ostfildern, using data from OpenStreetMap, licence CC-BY-SA 2.0 (28–29, 33, 41, 46, 48, 51, 60–61, 74–75, 86–87)
Cover design and pull-out map cover design: bilekjaeger_Kreativagentur with Zukunftswerkstatt, Stuttgart
Page design: Langenstein Communication GmbH, Ludwigsburg

Heartwood Publishing credits:
Translated from the German by Sophie Blacksell Jones, Jennifer Walcoff Neuheiser and Samantha Riffle
Editors: Rosamund Sales, Kate Michell, Felicity Laughton
Prepress: Summerlane Books, Bath
Printed in India

MARCO POLO AUTHOR

RALF JOHNEN has spent a large proportion of his life in Cologne. As a professional newspaper journalist, he appreciates the city's compact size and its central location in the heart of Europe. He loves strolling through the city's varied districts considering to what extent 21st-century Cologne has preserved its unique characteristics. He's certain that the city's brewhouses and carnival traditions will always be a source of fascination for visitors.

DOS & DON'TS

HOW TO AVOID SLIP-UPS & BLUNDERS

DON'T PUSH IN
The locals are generally good-natured, but they won't be happy if you shoulder them aside during carnival in order to get to the front of a pub queue or to the best spot for the carnival procession.

DO USE PUBLIC TRANSPORT
Driving and parking in the city is a frustrating experience, so make use of Cologne's public transport network, which is comprehensive, efficient and good value – the U-Bahn (metro) is definitely the best way to get around when you're tired of walking.

DON'T DROP YOUR CHEWING GUM
Dropping used chewing gum on the street is strictly prohibited in Cologne. If you're caught, you're liable for a 35-euro fine.

DON'T GET THE NAME WRONG
At the *Brauhaus* it doesn't matter if the waiter in the blue jacket is called Albert or Peter: simply call him *Köbes* (pronounced: cur-bes) and certainly never *Herr Ober* (waiter).

DON'T ORDER TEA IN A BRAUHAUS
The response is likely to be: "We are in a pub, not a sanatorium!" The *Köbes* will react just as rudely if you order a glass of mulled wine. But the worst thing you can possible do is to order an *Altbier*, a beer that comes from Düsseldorf.